*A Future for*
*SOCIALISM*

# A Future for SOCIALISM

Bryan Gould

*Additional research by Charles Seaford*

JONATHAN CAPE
THIRTY-TWO BEDFORD SQUARE
LONDON

First published 1989
© Bryan Gould 1989
Jonathan Cape Ltd, 32 Bedford Square, London WC1B 3SG

A CIP catalogue record for this book
is available from the British Library

ISBN 0–224–02710–7 (hardback)
     0–224–02728–X (paperback)

Printed in Great Britain by
Mackays of Chatham PLC

*for Gill*

# Contents

FOREWORD     xi

I THE SOCIALIST RETREAT     1
The Crosland analysis     1
The lost ground     2
The revival of the Right     3
The demise of Keynesianism     5
The internationalisation of capital     6
The new capitalism     9
The end of Fordism?     15
Prisoners of the past     18
The housing mistake     19
The failure to adapt     20
Internal behaviour     23
Accidental factors     24

2 THE THATCHER LEGACY     26
The moral climate     26
Economic failure     28
The power of international capital     32
The reinforcement of privilege     37
The new technology     41
The concentration of power in the media     42
The assault on freedom     45
Excessive centralisation     50
Thatcherite blind spots     52

3 THE SOCIALIST RESPONSE     55
Grounds for hope     55
A socialism for the 1990s     58
The diffusion of power     60
The power to choose     64

The importance of society 67
Looking forward 72

4   SOCIALISM AND WEALTH CREATION 74
Attitudes to success 74
Full employment 77
Organising the economy 80
An industrial strategy 85
The trade unions 89

5   THE ROLE OF THE MARKET 94
A false argument 94
The advantages of the market 95
The market's pretensions 96
The market's inefficiencies 98
The need to intervene 108

6   DIFFUSING POWER THROUGH OWNERSHIP 113
The role of private property 113
Does ownership matter? 118
The experience of public ownership 120
The major utilities 123
How should public ownership be achieved? 126

7   DEMOCRATISING THE ENTERPRISE 134
Common ownership for the whole economy 134
Employee ownership 137
Esops 143
Changes in company law and industrial 149
    democracy
Pension funds 153
Wage-earner funds 154
Regional enterprise boards 156

8   EMPOWERING THE CONSUMER 158
The importance of consumption 158
Regulating the utilities 159
Maintaining market competition 161
Consumer ownership 163
Credit unions 164

Community businesses 165
Protecting the consumer 166
Making collective provision more responsive 167

9 DIFFUSING POLITICAL POWER 173
Is democracy enough? 173
Electoral reform 176
A Bill of Rights 178
The nature of political power 180

10 A SOCIALISM FOR THE FUTURE 184

BIBLIOGRAPHY 188
INDEX 189

# Foreword

The Thatcherite experiment is now approaching its end. The judgment to be made of it is, I believe, necessarily a harsh one, but one point can be conceded – Margaret Thatcher was right to recognise that Britain and British politics had to escape from the cul-de-sac into which the post-war consensus had led us.

That consensus had accepted a number of fundamentally pessimistic assumptions about the state of Britain and the sort of future we could expect. It was widely agreed that we had little or no independent scope in foreign policy, and that the best we could hope for was to operate as an adjunct to American policy. It was accepted that we had little chance of remaining a viable economy, notwithstanding the successful experience of economies as diverse as Japan, Austria and Sweden, and had no option but to seek integration into a wider European economy, however onerous or unsuitable the terms we were offered might be. It was believed that there was no solution to our endemic problems of declining international competitiveness except through deflation and financial orthodoxy, however damaging those policies might be to our productive capacity.

Mrs Thatcher, without in any sense addressing these particular issues, at least recognised that the comfortable but inexorable decline – in comparative terms – which was the necessary consequence of these attitudes could not be tolerated. She was at least determined to shake things up, and to try to regenerate the British economy and to reinvigorate British society.

In this, she has of course failed miserably. The medicine she prescribed was in many respects worse than the cure. Her mistake was to look backwards to our past for solutions which might have been suited to a more primitive economy but which were totally inappropriate to the needs of an economy struggling to make gains in competitiveness in an era of new technology.

What she has done, however, is to ensure that there can be no going back. Neither the country nor the Left can return to the old assumptions and ways of doing things. The Left in particular can no longer bumble along, confident that we can afford mistakes, indulging self-delusion, giving unnecessary hostages to fortune, not facing up to problems, ignoring the legitimate demands of our supporters, believing that we can rely on a sort of historical inevitability and need not therefore try too hard.

All those illusions have been swept aside. The result is that, while the Thatcher experiment will be seen in the longer term to have failed, its most lasting achievement might well prove to be one which was least intended – a stimulus to the revival of the Left. Its real role may well have been as the necessary precursor to a new range of socialist policies and attitudes which will take us into the twenty-first century.

We are still too close to Thatcherism for it to be easy to make final judgments; it is a record whose interpretation is naturally still the subject of lively political controversy. When the smoke of battle finally clears, however, I believe that the Thatcher years will be seen to have been full of sound and fury but to have signified very little. The failure will be seen to have been a failure to grapple successfully with the issues which really confront us so that, by pursuing false trails, we have lost ground – a failure not only in terms of practical politics but also – crucially – a failure of ideology.

The practical failures will become very clear in retrospect. They have left us with a society which is less cohesive, a meaner moral climate, a less democratic system of government, and an economy which is woefully ill-prepared for the stern tests to come. These practical consequences of Thatcherite government reflect a wider and deeper failure – a failure of the ideology which took us backward to the nineteenth rather than forward to the twenty-first century.

It is the explicitly ideological nature of Thatcherite government which ensures that its failure must be judged in similar terms. The belief that 'there is no such thing as society', that the market must always prevail, that government has few responsibilities other than holding the ring, that individual greed is the only mainspring and guarantor of social advance, that the community need feel no concern for its less advantaged members, have all been thoroughly tested over more than a decade. If they have not worked, even in terms of their stated objectives, it is the ideology which must now bear the brunt of the criticism.

If I am right in this, and also right in my contention that the option of simply reverting to the doctrines and policies of the 1960s and 1970s is no longer open to the Left, the Thatcherite failure offers us the chance of escaping from the polarised, all-or-nothing, black-or-white nature of political argument in this country. That argument has been more a matter of posturing than of proper political analysis, but in the past this posturing successfully convinced the British people that they had to choose between a rampant and selfish individualism on the one hand and an antithetical insistence on bureaucratic inertia on the other.

That arid dichotomy is no longer possible. We now have the chance and duty, as socialists, to show that our socialism is not just the polar opposite of everything that has happened – good and bad – in the 1980s. We can show that we do not have to choose between efficiency and compassion, between individual achievement and community responsibility, between the market and collective provision, between freedom and equality, but that socialism offers us a synthesis of these aims and values. The Thatcherite ideological failure means we can offer socialism as a superior theory, which is not a reversion to a pre-Thatcherite society but which overtakes, leapfrogs and outdates Thatcherism because it is better suited to the needs of society and the aspirations of individuals in the coming century.

The socialism which I describe in this book is an empowering and liberating socialism which gives proper emphasis to the constructive potential of the relationship between the individual and society. It recognises that the basic political questions arise from this relationship, and that socialism is defined by the insight it provides into how this relationship can, if understood and arranged properly, both strengthen society and help to realise the full potential of each individual.

It is a socialism which proclaims the traditional virtues of social organisation, collective provision, and community responsibility. It argues that they are attainable not in antithesis to individual enterprise, freedom, choice and autonomy but as necessary concomitants of the achievement of those objectives. It is, in other words, a socialism which bases itself on the familiar doctrines of equality and social justice in their own right, but also shows how they are essential if each individual is to enjoy true freedom.

It is a socialism which enables us to align ourselves with the aspirations of each individual. We are no longer cut off from sharing with our natural supporters their personal ambitions for greater achievement and success, because we can show how these are to be attained only with the support and encouragement of social organisation; and we can give them a proper and wider value because we recognise the importance to society of the contribution made by each individual and the social as well as individual need to maximise that contribution.

We are also able to make full use of individual enterprise and the market mechanism because we understand both the benefits they can bring and the dangers they involve. We do not have to choose between market and non-market solutions; we can use them as appropriate to the achievement of our wider goals of diffusing power, strengthening society and helping the individual towards fulfilment.

A balanced understanding of the respective roles of individual and collective enterprise also enables us to make the most of both, in terms of strengthening the national economy and raising standards of living in the widest sense. We do not have to pin all our hopes on the drive for personal aggrandisement while deliberately refusing to make the longer-term and wider provision which only the organised community can make, any more than we need to eschew the dynamism and drive of the individual in the interests of ensuring that the state plays its proper role in economic development.

A socialism that consciously encourages both the individual and the community, the market and collective provision, to do what each is best at doing, will be better attuned to the needs of a competitive economy moving into the twenty-first century than any *laissez-faire* policy or state bureaucracy could possibly be. It is socialist policies which will secure the necessary investment in the essential building blocks of economic success and ensure that the economy serves the national interest, as well as harnessing the dynamism and innovation of a properly regulated market. It is that synthesis of individual enterprise and community planning and organisation which provides the basis of an economic and industrial policy which is far superior to a blind reliance on market forces. The diffusion of power in the economic sphere, by giving working people the maximum control over their working lives, will also encourage economic advance.

Many of these themes are taken up and developed in Labour's recently published Policy Review. This book is not intended as an alternative formulation; the Policy Review is comprehensive and policy-oriented, whereas the present book provides an individual account of the thinking that underlies just one person's contribution to the reappraisal of where we stand now. I hope, however, that it will provide – like the Policy Review – further evidence that socialism, far from being defunct, is full of vibrant life and is an essential passport to our future.

# CHAPTER ONE

## *The Socialist Retreat*

### THE CROSLAND ANALYSIS

When Anthony Crosland published *The Future of Socialism* in 1956, it was possible for him to argue that the socialist project had been largely achieved in this country. Many of his contemporaries disagreed with him, but he could nevertheless marshal an impressive case. The modern reader of Crosland must be struck, not so much by the detail of the case he argues, as by the sense of achievement he describes – and the invulnerability and permanence claimed for that achievement.

For Crosland, capitalism had confounded Marx by resolving its problems, and, in particular, had unlocked the secret of economic growth. There was now more than enough to go round – enough to give a rising share of the national income to labour without prejudicing the capitalist investment, enough for exports and investment as well as for increasing consumption, enough to finance ever-improving public services and welfare benefits without unduly limiting personal consumption through excessive taxes.

British capitalism had done well by Britain. The British economy was internationally competitive. Such sacrifices as had to be made were made – if not equally – at least more fairly than before, and the share of the national wealth taken by wages had risen. Poverty had declined and the achievements of the Welfare State were not likely to be challenged.

These changes had been partly the cause and partly the consequence of a loss of faith and confidence on the part of capitalists themselves. They no longer hymned the virtues of *laissez-faire* and the free market. They were now concerned with what was 'fair' and 'reasonable'. They recognised that they had lost power, on the one hand to the new technocrats and professional managers, who had no personal stake in ownership and profits as such, and on the other hand to organised labour, which, through the trade unions, now wielded considerable political as well as industrial power.

The State, too, through the extension of the public sector, had acquired power at the expense of the private capitalist. Nationalisation had placed large and important parts of the economy in the hands of public sector managers rather than private sector capitalists. The Welfare State, and the National Health Service (NHS) in particular, had displaced the market and demonstrated the great advantages of collective provision.

Above all was the over-arching achievement of full employment. It was full employment that produced the national wealth with which social reforms could be afforded. It was full employment that had decisively swung the balance in favour of labour and against capital. It was full employment that had transformed political sentiment and public opinion, to such a degree that, Crosland believed, if unemployment through a deficiency of demand were ever to re-appear, 'then the full employment theme would provide all the dynamic needed to sweep Labour back into power'.

THE LOST GROUND

Thirty years later, those comfortable certainties seem not so much misplaced as laughable. The catalogue of socialist achievement, seeming to Crosland to have been set in concrete, has shattered. The pillars of socialist society appear to have crumbled – and with them, the mood, the confidence, that we had embarked upon a journey to socialism on which there was no turning back.

Crosland's conclusion that Britain was no longer a capitalist country now seems remarkable, not so much because it was wrong at the time as because it has been so thoroughly and comprehensively invalidated by subsequent experience. It is true that the long-awaited Marxist crisis of capitalism has again been deferred, despite the stock market crash of October 1987, and that the capitalist economy continues to deliver – after a brief hiccup in the early 1980s – rising living standards, at least to a majority. Britain's economic experience in the 1970s and

1980s does, however, show that the Croslandite faith that we had discovered the secret of sustainable growth was misplaced. The British economy, notwithstanding the short-term benefits of North Sea oil, is no nearer to resolving the endemic problems of inflation, trade deficits and declining competitiveness that were already becoming apparent when Crosland was writing.

The most obvious departure, however, from the course that Crosland had so confidently predicted has been the revival of morale on the Right. The 'cautious Peelites', whom Crosland identified as being in charge of the Tory Party and as being unlikely to challenge the achievements of the Attlee Government, have been replaced by a Thatcherite leadership bent on dismantling and eliminating every last vestige of socialism.

Inequality and poverty have both increased. The advance of the public sector has been not only halted but reversed. The Welfare State has been weakened and undermined. The capitalist ethics of the free market, private property, self-help, competition and *laissez-faire* are rampant. The trade unions have been emasculated and sidelined, and have been joined in their enfeebled condition by other former bastions of socialist consciousness such as local government.

Most significant, the unemployment that Crosland so confidently regarded as a thing of the past, has not only re-emerged in greater dimensions than before; it has subsisted for a decade, and reversed all the advances in the condition of labour that Crosland had identified as a consequence of full employment. It has also been tolerated. Far from calling forth the 'dynamic' that would sweep Labour back to power, unemployment has produced an uncertain response from the Labour Party and has proved to be little obstacle to the re-election of Tory governments in 1983 and 1987.

THE REVIVAL OF THE RIGHT

Why have the Croslandite analysis and prediction been so comprehensively disproved? Why has the serene confidence of the 1950s been replaced by the doubts and uncertainty of the 1980s? What happened to transform the seemingly immutable socialist consensus into the rampant individualism we see in Britain today? What went wrong?

There are, of course, some easy answers to this fundamental question. Like most easy answers to difficult questions, they are wrong. In some sections of the Left, the answer proffered is that all would have been well but for the failure of Labour governments and the betrayals by the Labour leadership. If only, so the argument runs, Labour had pursued the path towards 'full-blooded socialism' more resolutely – if only we had offered more by way of nationalisation and central planning – then the British people would have responded with gratitude and enthusiasm, and the Thatcherite nightmare need never have happened.

On the Right, the simple-minded answer is equally implausible. According to this view, the country was saved from socialism by the arrival of Superwoman, who first converted the Tory Party and then the country to her non-socialist vision.

Neither of these explanations takes proper account of the fact that political developments in Britain have been just a part of what has been played out on a much wider stage, and that the factors that influence those political developments are much more complex than the policies and views of individual politicians.

It is not necessary to devalue the impressive political and electoral achievement of Margaret Thatcher in order to make good the claim that she is at least as much the beneficiary as the progenitor of political change in this country. She has been resolute and skilful in seizing her opportunities; and it would be surprising if a dominant prime minister had not had some influence on events, moods and attitudes. Yet it remains true that this Prime Minister has ridden the wave rather than created it; she has helped it along rather than been its source.

Where, then, did the world-wide swing to the Right originate, if not in the breast of Margaret Thatcher? It is tempting to say that the swing followed the natural pendulum of fashion as much as anything else, and this contention has some plausibility, at least in purely British terms.

In the 1950s, memories of the Second World War were still fresh. The determination not to return to the bad old days of social division and unemployment, the experience of working together – women as well as men – for the common good in the war effort, the recognition that it was possible to meet national objectives through planning and mobilising common resources, the great achievements of the post-war Government – these were the dominant political attitudes.

But inevitably, in the years that followed, those perceptions dimmed. The achievements were tarnished by practical failures and began to look less sustainable; the price to be paid for them began to weigh heavier; the aspirations were harder to maintain; the once-discredited alternatives looked more alluring. There is a sense in which political and practical failure – unlike success, which is often taken for granted – is cumulative and mounts in the balance sheet. And there are never any final battles in politics.

During the 1960s and 1970s, the great benefits of full employment and the Welfare State were, in the public estimation, reduced in value. Economic problems it was thought had been overcome – of inflation, the balance of payments, competitiveness – re-emerged. New problems – of bureaucracy, of trade union power, of an insensitivity to consumer needs – arose. There was a growing and uneasy recognition that Britain was failing to keep pace with other countries, and a natural tendency to blame the prevailing orthodoxy for that failure. The pendulum was beginning to swing.

## THE DEMISE OF KEYNESIANISM

This swing was given greater impetus by the oil price shock of the early 1970s. The inflationary stimulus and the disruption to world economic growth and trade delivered by the sudden hike in oil and other commodity prices seemed finally to invalidate Keynesian economics. Governments could no longer guarantee growth and full employment by means of deficit financing and public spending, judicious intervention and fine-tuning. Full employment and the Welfare State were thought to exact a heavy price in terms of inflation and efficiency. 'There is no such thing as a free lunch' became the favourite economic nostrum.

The long-defunct ideas of classical economics re-appeared in the guise of monetarism. The doctrines of monetarism appeared to offer certainty in an uncertain world, and a limited but manageable role to governments that had retired in confusion from trying to grapple with mounting economic problems. Monetarism appealed in particular to the financial markets, which found themselves suddenly cast as the final arbiters of economic policy, and to right-wing politicians, who correctly recognised it as a political rather than an economic doctrine.

Governments and parties of the Left were swept up in the new enthusiasm for simple certainties. It was a Labour Government in Britain that in 1976 tacitly conceded that full employment was either no longer attainable or was attainable at too high a price. It was a Labour Prime Minister who told the Party Conference that it was not possible to 'spend our way out of a recession'. It was a Labour Chancellor who conducted his policy on the unspoken assumption that policy had to be what the money markets demanded, who adjusted policy in the light of the monthly £M3 figures, and who declared in the late 1970s that 'We are all monetarists now'.

The concession that full employment could no longer be the central objective of economic policy was of profound significance. It fundamentally undermined the post-war accommodation of capital and labour. Labour – even organised labour – was dealt a severe blow. The balance of advantage in the labour market swung decisively in favour of the employer.

The implications were wider still. If Government was now powerless to intervene in the workings of the labour market, and if economic policy as a whole was now to be defined in terms of what was acceptable to the money markets – if, in other words, markets alone were to determine outcome in these central parts of the economy – why should markets not also prevail in other spheres of policy? If markets were to be trusted to produce the right results in economic policy, why not in education, or housing, or health care? So it was that the Left sold the pass and lost the argument.

THE INTERNATIONALISATION OF CAPITAL

Other factors also had a powerful impact. In the 1950s, it was possible for Crosland to analyse the state of Britain with virtually no reference to our place in the world economy. By the 1970s, all that had changed. Our entry into the EEC confirmed and hastened the conclusion that British economic performance could no longer be evaluated in domestic terms alone.

The immediate consequence was that the battle that labour appeared to have won in terms of the Crosland analysis, and that had produced rising wages both absolutely and as a proportion of the national wealth, was now seen to continue, but on a much wider battle-field – and one that was much more advantageous to capital. Powerful organised labour could exploit a politically dictated full employment in order to push up wages and restrict the capitalist's return; but it was now perceived that this could be done only at the expense of declining competitiveness and a falling world market share.

The message that labour could take the golden eggs only by emaciating the golden goose was a congenial one for capital, but it was also echoed on the revolutionary Left, as a means of demonstrating that capitalism could not be managed in the interests of labour. Capital itself had, of course, already taken the necessary defensive action, by escaping the constraints imposed by national governments and becoming international. The process exemplified by the establishment of the EEC continued with the further removal of barriers to trade, the growing influence of the multinationals, the imminence of a single European market and the creation of a global twenty-four-hour capital market.

The growing perception that Britain is now just a part of a single world economy has worked very much to the advantage of capital and of the Right. It has enabled capital to deploy the ultimate weapon against labour – the threat to move capital, and with it investment, employment and living standards, to those parts of the world economy where labour costs are lowest, labour most compliant and the obligations of capital least onerous. What does it avail a workforce to force a wage increase or an improvement in conditions from an employer if the consequence is that jobs are lost, either because the employer then moves elsewhere or because the apparently inexorable laws of international competition dictate that the jobs are no longer competitive and the capacity must be closed down?

This has been a powerful weapon against labour, but it has also been effective when directed against national governments

– particularly those of an interventionist bent. Capital, with the freedom to roam world-wide, has naturally gravitated towards those regimes that are sympathetic to it. Governments of the Left have been easily portrayed as anti-business, and consequently threatening to jobs and living standards, and their ability to defend labour, or even the national interest, has accordingly diminished.

This reduced ability of governments and trade unions to resist capital has been accompanied by a growing sense of apathy and powerlessness on the part of labour. Workers have become fearful for their jobs and critical of those whom they would in other circumstances have regarded as their protectors and allies, but who are now seen as threatening their livelihoods through excessive and unsuccessful militancy.

These hard lessons in the iron law of the market have had a profound political impact. Nothing could have been more conducive to a loss of confidence on the Left and an easy ride for governments of the Right. The Left has found itself in a dilemma because it has not been possible either to deny or to resist these developments without opting out of the world economy altogether. While the siege economy – insulated against world competition by trade barriers, exchange controls and so on – may have some attractions, and some adherents on the far Left, it is hardly a basis for widespread popular appeal when the electorate understandably fear that it will result in hardship and lower living standards.

Yet once it is accepted that Britain has no option but to compete in world markets, including our own, then much else follows. Not only must labour costs and labour practices be brought into line; so, too, it is argued, must inflation rates. This means that monetary policy must be harmonised, and, following that, fiscal policy. All experience shows that once a particular monetary target is accepted as paramount, all other instruments of policy must eventually be subordinated to the achievement of that target. Labour governments from Ramsay MacDonald to Jim Callaghan, and socialist governments abroad – like the first Mitterand Government in France – have discovered how damaging this can be to socialist aspirations.

If the prevailing international orthodoxy – and therefore the basis of harmonisation – is a right-wing emphasis on financial orthodoxy, on monetary discipline, on free markets, on compliant labour, then it appears that this is the basis on which we too must harmonise. Again, the whole thrust of international developments has been to favour the Right and handicap the Left.

The dilemma is particularly acute for a would-be Government of the Left in a country like Britain, which has been losing ground in comparative economic terms. The natural course of such a Government would be to use the instruments of intervention and regulation – investment incentives and controls, regulated trade, regional policy, strategic help to industry and so on – to stimulate the economy, build on strength, protect weakness. But the right-wing free market consensus and the pressure to harmonise on that basis mean that these measures are no longer available to any Government, let alone an interventionist one.

This means that the substantial burden of restoring lost competitiveness must rest primarily on labour. The placing of that burden – both politically and economically – on the shoulders of the working class, forcing them to make all the sacrifices and concessions to capital as the consequence of apparently inexorable laws of economics, is again extremely congenial to the Right and debilitating to the Left.

THE NEW CAPITALISM

Crosland may have been wrong in asserting that Britain was no longer a capitalist country, but he was on firmer ground in declaring that modern experience had comprehensively invalidated much of the Marxist prediction as to the future course of capitalism. Contrary to Marx's analysis, capitalism has proved remarkably robust in surviving its problems. It has delivered growth and rising living standards to most people, not just to a tiny minority of capitalists. The exploitation and alienation of labour, undeniably still a factor, have not created a proletariat ripe for revolution. Class is not seen by most people as the prime determinant of their needs, interests and attitudes.

On the other hand, the capitalism that Crosland described as having been transformed out of all recognition has proved remarkably resilient, and has retained and revived its essential characteristics to an extent that would have astonished him. The power of capital – to own, control, employ labour, take the profits, dictate to governments – remains and seems likely to grow. Modern economies seem likely to become more rather than less dependent on capital. Labour seems likely to become less important to the wealth-creating process, and the claim of labour on its product to become even less compelling.

The questions of who owns capital and what rights and responsibilities go with its provision remain therefore of essential importance to the socialist, and, indeed, to all political activists. In the early days of capitalism, the answers to these questions were quite straightforward. The only people who had capital were the landowners and traders. They were the only people with the economic power to put together the components of production – the land, the equipment, the raw materials, the labour, the access to markets and so on – and it seemed to follow naturally that the holders of this monopoly of economic power should be regarded as the owners of its product. The product was itself then transformed back into capital, thus reinforcing the monopoly of capital and the economic power enjoyed by the individual and private capitalist.

Capitalism on that model was a matter of individual capitalists competing with each other for markets and each engaged in a common exploitation of labour. The power and rights of each individual capitalist derived from his or her individual ownership of capital.

The picture today is very different. The modern generators of capital are not, in general, individual capitalists. Surprisingly little of the investment capital required by the wealth-creating process today is derived from the return on capital invested by individual capitalists. By far the most important source of capital in modern Britain is ordinary people, saving for their old age and retirement. It is the savings of millions of such ordinary people, collected and organised in pension funds, or in life insurance policies, that provide the major source of new equity capital for British industry.

A further major source of capital is not real wealth at all, but credit, created by the banking system. Private sector credit, for both investment and consumption, is being created by the banks and financial institutions at a record rate, and is increasing by about £50 billion each year – over 10 per cent of the Gross Domestic Product (GDP). Again, this capital (when it is used as such) is not generated and owned by – in the ordinary sense – individual capitalists. It is organised and controlled by institutions and corporations that do not belong to any one individual or group of individuals, and is provided by them to the wealth-creators, who, usually on a corporate basis as well, own and control industrial and commercial enterprises.

If capital is no longer generated from within the resources of individual capitalists, and is then organised, controlled and utilised by institutions and corporations that are not owned by individual capitalists, what, then, is the modern significance of the ownership of capital? If we accept for the moment the capitalist principle that ownership of capital carries with it necessarily the rights of ownership and control, who is entitled to those rights?

On the face of it, it might be argued that those rights should pass to the millions of people who contribute their savings, and to the community in whose name and for whose purposes credit is created. If that had happened, we might already be talking about an economic system that was in some senses owned by the community. Yet that apparently straightforward application of the capitalist principle has manifestly not been made.

Control, if not ownership, of those billions of pounds' worth of savings and credit has been ceded to those who own and control the financial institutions. They cannot claim to be capitalists in the usual sense, because they do not themselves create or own the capital that they control. They exercise control because the community permits them to do so. Nor are they capitalists in the sense that they use their control over capital to buy and own the wealth-creating process. Neither the banks, which provide capital by way of overdraft, nor the pension funds and insurance companies, which buy equity, own, in the ordinary sense, the enterprises to which they provide capital. It is true that the ownership of equity does carry with it the rights of ownership; but the institutions do not generally buy enough shares in any one company to give them the usual rights of ownership and control over that company. Indeed, it is the essence of the criticism usually directed at the financial institutions that they fight shy of playing the role of owner, and do not therefore involve themselves to the extent that they should, preferring to change investments rather than improve efficiency if the investment proves disappointing.

This is not to say that the institutions do not exercise any power. On the contrary, they exercise very considerable power, but of a diffuse and negative kind. Their real power derives not so much from the direct rights of ownership as from the implied and often real threat to move their capital elsewhere, or to play a decisive role in takeover battles.

If financial institutions do not exercise the powers of ownership, who does? The answer seems to be the tautological one that the owners of the industrial or commercial enterprise do. Their ownership seems, in other words, not to depend on the provision of the capital (except, perhaps, in some sense of providing the original capital); rather, the provision of new capital seems to accrue to and reinforce ownership.

If ownership does not seem to depend on the provision of capital, on what does it depend? What special contribution does the modern owner make to justify the unique rights of ownership?

The answer is an elusive one. Ownership does not now depend on the provision of any particular skill, since the owner will be able to buy in that skill, at whatever price may be appropriate, and yet remain owner. This is true even of the skill involved in organising the enterprise as a whole – the putting together of all the elements of production – which is often thought to be the special responsibility and prerogative of ownership, and to justify the rights of ownership. It is quite possible, and indeed is frequently the case, that the owners have little to do with the actual running of their enterprise, but merely employ those who do. It is hard to escape the conclusion that the owners own because our law, particularly our company law, has developed a concept of ownership and someone has to do it.

Who, then are these owners, who provide neither particular skills nor the bulk of the capital their enterprises need?

In some cases they are easily identified, at least in terms of putting names to them. A Robert Maxwell or a Tiny Roland is clearly 'in charge' and decides the fate of billions of pounds. To all intents and purposes, in terms of the control they exercise, these individuals are the owners of their vast empires.

Yet they exercise that control, and the rights of ownership, because institutional and corporate investors – and, through them, millions of small savers – cede that power to them. No one believes that Robert Maxwell has himself created the billions of pounds' worth of assets he now controls. He exercises that power because he has access to and control over assets placed at his disposal by institutional investors, who in turn have organised the savings of millions of ordinary people. Robert Maxwell is enabled to extend his power as an individual capitalist by using his access to capital (including credit) to acquire further assets, which in turn provide him with the base to attract to him the use of yet further assets.

The process is less the one Marx described, of the individual capitalist using his personal wealth to exploit labour through appropriating the surplus value of their productive work, than of acquisition and organisation – a matter of controlling factors such as access to markets. It is a process which occurs by virtue of the fact that a given person or organisation is already an owner, and is thereby judged a safe repository for other people's capital.

Not every enterprise, of course, is owned or controlled by a Robert Maxwell. Ownership and control are not usually concentrated in quite that way in individual hands. It is usually a matter of corporate control and ownership – of groups of lesser-known Robert Maxwells exercising collectively the same range of powers, which are rather more flamboyantly deployed by Maxwell himself.

Who are these people? Like Robert Maxwell, they are not essentially individual capitalists in the old sense. They may be capitalists in the sense that they invest their individual wealth in capitalist enterprises, but this is usually, in the context of the vast sums of investment capital now required by industry, on a relatively small scale. They are, in other words, characterised not so much by the ownership of capital as by their access to and control over it.

These owners therefore constitute a collective capitalism

rather different from the individual capitalism described by Marx. They are, as a class, the people who crop up time and time again in the boardrooms of our major companies, and who also populate the boardrooms of the major financial institutions. Their significance stems from their membership of that corporate culture, and only secondarily from their role as individual owners and contributors of capital.

It is this corporate culture of capitalism that should now be engaging our attention. It is in many ways a more formidable phenomenon than the one Marx described, where individuals exploit the workers as a means of securing individual economic success.

It is a culture more pervasive and comprehensive than anything Marx had envisaged, and its boundaries are also much harder to define. Marx had no doubt what a capitalist did and what his role was, because he had to fulfil a defined Marxist role in the economy. Today's capitalist has no such easily identified characteristics.

This is not to accept the Crosland thesis that power has passed from the capitalist to the technocrat and professional manager. Such people do exist, and they do exercise real power. But the notion that they are easily separable from the capitalist class and that they are the inheritors of capitalist power is not accurate, if only because they have themselves become absorbed by the capitalist culture. They are, as much as anyone is today, capitalists themselves.

There are many people in society today whom Marx would not have recognised as capitalists – indeed, whom Marx would not have recognised at all, since they are neither the exclusive owners of capital nor members of an oppressed and exploited class. They are the people whom the British Communist Party describe as occupying 'contradictory class locations' – people who feel, rightly or wrongly, that they have some sort of stake in the productive process (other than that of wage slaves) and who have to some extent thereby absorbed some part of the capitalist culture, without in any sense meeting the Marxist definition of what it means to be a capitalist.

To some extent, this downward diffusion of capitalist power – so that it is no longer the exclusive preserve of a small group of individual capitalists – is a welcome and perhaps inevitable reflection of the point made earlier, that the modern providers of capital are the millions of small savers, whom capitalist principle would identify as the new owners of industry.

On the other hand, however, it could also be regarded as a defence mechanism, a necessary concession, on the part of the capitalist class, which enables them to retain the bulk of their power by making a concession that is largely an illusion. They have secured the allegiance of many more people in society to the capitalist culture by sharing a part of their power, but they have been careful at the same time to retain the real concentration of power in their own hands. Indeed, at the same time as the penumbra of power has been extended so as to embrace many more people, its essential concentration has increased, so that the heartland of the modern economy is now in fewer hands than ever before.

It is this allegiance to capitalist culture that falsifies the Crosland thesis. Many managers, self-employed people, small shareholders, may have an insignificant personal stake in industry, but are nevertheless part of the capitalist structure, ethic and culture. They help to insulate those who exercise real power against the claims and criticisms of those whom Marx expected to bring about the revolution of the proletariat. They provide new recruits to the political values of the Right and models for others to emulate.

THE END OF FORDISM?

There are other changes in the way our economy operates that are said to have acted against what are usually thought to be the workers' interests. It is argued by some that the Labour Party has been and is the political product of an industrial economy whose day is past and that has now been superseded by an economy and society to which the Labour Party is increasingly irrelevant. Whether this perception is substantially true or not, its wide acceptance is one of the factors that contribute to an image of Labour as irremediably outdated.

The old order is the 'Fordism' of the national economy – of mass production, of well-defined and static economic relationships, of industrial trade unions, of large factories and the strict division of labour. It is the society of class conflict and mass housing, standardisation and bureaucracy. It is the birthplace of the Labour movement and the familiar terrain of Labour activity throughout this century.

But, so the argument runs, while the Labour movement digs in, ready for trench warfare in defence of the old order, Fordism is – at least in part – being transformed. The new terrain is that of high technology, of decentralisation, of small firms, of flexible work practices and non-unionised labour, of computers and information technology. It is a future of diversity and flexibility, of internationalisation on the one hand and designer labels on the other.

It is here that the political battles of the future – indeed, of the present – will be fought and won. This is what many people see as the future course of our economy and society and it is here that Labour, with its reliance on class-based politics and its close association with the trade unions, is ill-equipped for the struggle. The trade unions, like Labour, are seen, according to this perception, as outdated institutions, wedded to old prac-tices, defensive of vested interests, resistant to change, male-dominated, confrontational in attitude, obstacles rather than aids to a more prosperous future.

For these reasons, Labour is seen as out of tune with the country's future. So far, Thatcherite Tories have looked to be more convincing guardians of our future, not necessarily because they were better prepared, or more intelligent, or ideologically more attuned to the new developments, but because political logic compelled them to find a new battle-field – one they must have been surprised as well as delighted to find uncontested while the Labour Party massed its troops on territory the Tories had long since abandoned.

This is undeniably a difficult area for the Labour Party. The notion of a painless and overnight conversion from something called Fordism to a quite different, post-Fordist, future may be a useful tool of analysis for academic or journalistic commenta-tors, but it is very far removed from the real world.

In that real world, large parts of a Fordist economy are still alive and well. Those who live and work in it still look to the Labour movement to represent their interests. The option of painlessly shucking off what might be regarded as the incubus of the past and addressing an exclusively post-Fordist future is simply not open to us.

On the other hand, the dangers of remaining frozen in time are equally real. It is very much in the Tory interest to portray Labour as irredeemably wedded to an industrial and class structure that is becoming less and less important or relevant. Our problem is to show that we are alert to the changes that are taking place, and well able to support and encourage them, without needing to abandon, either explicitly or implicitly, our traditional constituencies.

We must, in other words, reject the post-Fordist thesis so far as it suggests that we must make some black-or-white, all-or-nothing choice between two polar opposites. The truth is that post-Fordism is part of the natural process of change. It owes very little to political developments, Thatcherite or otherwise. It occurs across a broad front, but piecemeal and at variable speed. It occurs as a continuum, rather than representing a sharp break with the past. So far as it is represented by new technology and new work methods, it is at least as much a feature of Fordist economic activity as of silicon valley. It is an integral part of the welcome but necessarily complex process of modernising our economy and decentralising power.

As on so many other issues, however, the Labour Party has found it hard to handle the process of change, partly because of our necessary commitment to our existing constituencies. Our difficulties have also arisen, though, because of an unwillingness to disentangle the issues. There is unfortunately no shortage of the sort of feeble-mindedness that dictates that a Tory claim to political territory, however desirable and important the territory may be, is of itself sufficient reason to abandon it as tainted.

Nowhere is this more true than on the question of how the economy and society are to be modernised. It is the Tories who now appear to point the way to the future, who pursue the politics of change, who are on the offensive in the name of modernisation. It is for these reasons that they have succeeded in establishing one of the paradoxes of modern British politics – that the Conservative Party is seen as an agent of change, while the Party of the radical Left appears to want only a return to the status quo ante.

PRISONERS OF THE PAST

The changes that have occurred in our industrial structures pose a genuine problem for the Labour Party. There is less excuse, however, for our refusal to adapt to other changes that have occurred and that we should have no difficulty in recognising and accepting.

Too often, we have demanded a luxury available to no one else – the luxury of ignoring change – and as a consequence we have played into the hands of our opponents. The divisions that matter in the Labour Party today are not those between Left and Right – terms which have an increasingly misleading and unhelpful meaning in today's politics in any case – but those between the fundamentalists and the radicals, the reactionaries and the modernisers. It is this tension, between those unwilling to move from the past and those who are ready to embrace the future, however uncertain and difficult it may be, that accounts for many of the Labour Party's problems and conflicts and that has disabled the Party as a counter-force to Thatcherism.

This has meant that the Party has at times found it difficult to keep up with the changing aspirations and interests of those who might be Labour voters. Too often, those in work, with rising incomes and savings, buying their own homes, seeking wider choices and more control over their own lives, have not been hailed as the pioneers of a greater and essentially socialist diversity and freedom, but have been condemned as class traitors.

We have been unwilling to acknowledge that rising living standards have led these people to demand a higher level of provision, with more individual choice and less willingness to accept a provision imposed by authority. Our attachment to the principle of collective provision has sometimes led us to deny the importance of consumer choice and satisfaction, and to emphasise the interests of producers rather than consumers.

We have also had difficulty with the concept of individual rights and choices. Our commitment to collective provision has made us suspicious of the new and sometimes strident calls for individual gratification. We have been unwilling to recognise that collective provision is merely a means to an end, and that any system of provision, whether collective or otherwise, that does not meet the needs and interests of the individuals it is meant to serve must be reckoned as a failure. Again, we have managed to convey a general air of at best grudging acceptance and at worst downright hostility to the new and welcome rise in the living standards of ordinary people.

By conveying a sense that to recognise and endorse these legitimate expectations and new standards is to betray those who cannot share them, we have often appeared to express a lack of sympathy with what ought to be clear socialist objectives – rising living standards and greater choice. For the sake of solidarity with the disadvantaged, we have alienated many natural Labour voters and have thus failed to obtain the political power that would best serve their interests.

THE HOUSING MISTAKE

The recent history of Labour policy on housing is a case in point. When the Tory Government began its programme of council house sales, often against the wishes of the relevant local authority and irrespective of local housing needs, the Labour Party rightly warned that the seeds of a major housing crisis were being sown. Not only was there something offensive about seeing major public assets, built up at the taxpayer's expense in order to meet a particular social need, being sold off at knock-down prices, without regard for the taxpayer's invest- ment or for the continuing importance of rented housing at reasonable rents; the sale of council houses, coupled with the failure to build new housing to rent in the public sector, also made it inevitable that many who could not afford to buy their own homes or to pay the high rents demanded by private landlords would be left unprovided for.

In many deprived areas, the consequence has been, not just an overall shortage of housing, but a loss from the housing stock of the family houses – the most desirable and therefore most easily saleable properties – which made proper management of the housing stock possible. The process by which a young couple would begin married life in a small flat, move into a maisonette as they had children, and then progress to a family house as the children grew up has ground to a halt. As a result, young mothers with growing children are trapped in high-rise blocks, with little prospect of escape.

This should have constituted a major indictment of the Tory Government. But because Labour chose, for ideological reasons, to concentrate on the form of tenure (a lawyer's concept, and rather a peculiar preoccupation for socialists), rather than on the supply of housing, the issue rebounded against us. By opposing council house sales, we appeared to be hostile to the whole concept of home ownership. By berating those who bought their council houses, we appeared to be denying to those who could not afford to buy on the open market the privileges the better off enjoyed as a matter of course. We found ourselves endorsing a form of income-based apartheid in housing of precisely the sort we vehemently and rightly opposed in health care and education.

Not surprisingly, too, those who found their home-owning aspirations threatened by the Labour Party concluded that they would do better to support Mrs Thatcher. We thereby lost the support of many voters on the council estates who would otherwise have voted Labour, and found ourselves debarred as a consequence from the political power that alone would have enabled us to deal with the real problem – the failure to build more houses.

The Party, of course, quickly learnt by its mistakes in housing policy and after 1983 adopted a much more realistic policy in this area, better attuned to the needs of Labour voters. But the damage had been done – and the thinking that produced the mistake remains to dog us.

THE FAILURE TO ADAPT

Issues of this sort will continue to arise in the future. More and more people, for example, will find themselves with capital sums for investment, not because they have suddenly chosen to become capitalists but because their home-owning parents will bequeath to them a substantial equity in the family home. More and more people will seek new patterns of employment, more flexible working conditions and opportunities for training and re-training throughout their working lives. New technology, such as inter-active fibre optic cabling, will revolutionise the way in which markets operate, so that they become more immediately responsive to individual requirements. We cannot afford to get caught in a time warp on issues of this sort, and to make the sort of mistake that so hurt us over housing.

The Labour Party's failure to adapt quickly enough to changing conditions has left us very vulnerable to the change in intellectual fashion. For years, in typically British fashion, the Labour Party showed little interest in ideas, preferring to rely on a pragmatic labourism and an obvious class interest, a general sense of being on the side of the underdog, and a faith in a sort of Fabian gradualism, which assumed that progressive forces were carrying us inexorably towards greater social justice.

The last decade has brought about a rude awakening from this self-delusion. Mrs Thatcher showed that the inexorable tide of social advance could be turned back. Reactionary ideas thought to be long dead reappeared with a horrifying vitality. The intellectual running was suddenly all being made on the Right. The one major post-war attempt at socialist analysis and prescription from within the Labour Party – Crosland's – was falsified by social and economic developments.

At the same time, the primitive (as opposed to Marxist) sense of class that had provided the social and political glue to hold the Labour Party together, granting it mainstream support and identity, ceased to hold. This is not to say that class does not remain a prominent and damaging feature of British society. It continues to waste human talent, close off opportunities, generate unfairness and destroy social harmony; the horizons of class victims are often so narrowed, and their expectations so reduced by its pernicious and all-pervasive influence, that they do not even question the injury they suffer.

The class war is, of course, still alive and well in the minds of those who feel their privileges to be threatened by working-class aspirations. The existence of a ruling class remains a prominent feature of British society, reinforced and insulated against change by social, educational, occupational and financial privilege, and offering the most pressing challenge to anyone who wishes to see a less hidebound and sclerotic society.

But class as a means of self-identification and as a motivator of political thought and action is no longer powerful enough to sustain the Labour Party. What was once the working class may still exist obviously enough for the sociologist, but as the bedrock of a political party it has become shifting sand. The British working class, largely as a consequence of social advances made possible by Labour governments, has neither the numbers nor the homogeneity to bring the Labour Party to power.

This is not a new problem. The working class, even at its most numerous and homogenous, has never provided unanimous support for the Labour Party; and Harold Wilson was only the most recent of Labour leaders to recognise the need both to attract support from beyond the working class and to discover, through 'the white heat of technology', the means of doing so. It is undeniable, however, that the class base of politics has eroded further through the 1980s, and that the gap between working-class values and the policies of the Labour Party has on many issues tended to widen.

So a Labour Party which found itself bereft of ideas, short of support, and with the intellectual and political tide running against it was suddenly thrown back – for want of anything else on offer – on a search for the old simple certainties. It is the natural response of a political party in trouble to seek to return to the basics; the problem was that even this turned out not to be as easy as it seemed. It meant, first of all, that we were constantly seeking out our past while Mrs Thatcher was surging forward; we were seen to be constantly looking backwards, defending the status quo, resisting change – not a very inspiring posture for a supposedly radical party of the Left.

Moreover, the only certainties available – simple or otherwise – were those on offer from Marxists of various sorts, who, as the tide of labourist support ebbed, became proportionately more important and influential. The difficulty was that an increasingly Marxist Labour Party – in tone if not in policy – found it more and more difficult to stay in touch with and retain the support of the voters who used to vote Labour but who were alienated by the sterility of Marxist doctrine.

This in turn led to a growing loss of confidence, and a sense that the Left had finally run out of ideas, and even of the will to govern. The 'winter of discontent' was not only a painful and damaging breach between the political and industrial wings of the movement; it also marked, as we can see in retrospect, an almost tangible weariness and defeatism in respect of the problems of government.

INTERNAL BEHAVIOUR

The alienation from the Labour Party felt by many traditional Labour voters was, of course, greatly aided by the well-publicised and often inaccurately reported (not to say completely invented) instances of 'looneyism' in which Labour local authorities and other Labour politicians were alleged to be involved. These could be largely dismissed as the work of political propagandists of the Right, but they certainly did their damage.

Other mistakes were made, however, for which responsibility could not so easily be disclaimed. For too long the Labour Party has regarded its own internal affairs as of intense interest to activists, but of little importance in deciding the Party's image with the wider public.

The point can be made by referring to polling evidence, which shows that many voters share what we regard as Labour values, yet nevertheless vote Tory. This is particularly true of women voters. The answer to this apparent paradox lies in further polling evidence showing that women in particular are alienated by attitudes of conflict and hostility, and that they associate these attitudes with the Labour Party. This suggests that they are more impressed by the way we actually behave and conduct our own internal affairs than by what we say or profess to be. In Opposition, we have no opportunity to show what we would do in Government; we are judged by how we conduct ourselves as an Opposition and by how we run our own affairs.

We may profess to be the Party of brotherly and sisterly love, but if we conduct ourselves in terms of conflict, and attack our opponents in terms of hatred and class warfare, the voters draw obvious conclusions. We may say that we are totally committed to democracy, but if the voters see that we arrange our own affairs along undemocratic lines and that individual members are denied the right to vote on important matters, they may take leave to disagree. We may say that we are opposed to racial and sex discrimination, but if it is clear that women or black people are inadequately represented in our Party institutions, the claim may seem rather hollow.


ACCIDENTAL FACTORS

This, then, is the post-Crosland history, and an account of some of the factors that explain the precipitate decline in the fortunes of the Left – a decline that Crosland had so confidently predicted would not happen. There were, of course, other factors as well – some depending on luck or accident, others deriving from or reinforcing the major developments already described. The personalities involved were also of some significance; things might have been marginally different if Margaret Thatcher or David Owen, for example, had not held their respective offices. The Falklands conflict was also fortuitous for the Tories, in the sense that it gave Mrs Thatcher the chance to show in a more favourable light qualities that had hitherto been regarded as profoundly unattractive.

The 1980s might also have been marginally less difficult for the Labour Party if the defection to the SDP had not taken place – not because the loss of the individuals concerned was of great importance, but because it signalled the Labour Party's failure to contend for the middle ground, offering the voters a 'moderate' anti-Thatcher option and raising questions over Labour's continuing viability as a Party of Government. In that sense, it was a symptom rather than a cause of Labour's problems.

Perhaps the most important accidental factor was North Sea oil. The temptation – particularly for those predisposed to yield to it – is to ascribe the Tory triumphs in 1983 and 1987 to the supposed revolution wrought by Mrs Thatcher. A much simpler explanation, however, lies to hand: British elections in modern times have generally been won and lost on what the Americans call 'pocket book' issues and a government that can deliver rising living standards to enough people generally has a head start at the polls.

Many commentators, at the time of the 1979 election, predicted that whoever won that election would, on the strength of the oil then coming on stream, remain in power for a decade. The Tory victories of 1983 and 1987 are, on one level, easily explicable on this ground. The accident of North Sea oil, for which Mrs Thatcher's Government can claim little or no credit, has nevertheless produced an additional £70 billion in tax revenues and £120 billion in extra national wealth, which no other Government has enjoyed and which has been used to relieve the balance of payments constraint which had so inhibited economic growth in the past. The Tory electoral triumphs of the 1980s undoubtedly owe a great deal to the fact that the Tories were lucky enough to be able to distribute the fruits of the North Sea to a grateful electorate.

# CHAPTER TWO

# *The Thatcher Legacy*

## THE MORAL CLIMATE

The need to counter-act and overcome the Thatcher legacy is perhaps the most pressing task we face. The legacy is a bitter one. There is the great increase in poverty, inequality and social disunity. There is the glorification of greed and selfishness, the tilting of the balance in favour of the already rich and powerful, and the subordination of the interests of others. There is the decline in social responsibility and concern. There is the growth of an authoritarian State to underpin the increasing concentration of economic power. There is the economic and social sclerosis, and the lack of preparedness for the competition we shall face in the modern world.

The task of healing and uniting the nation is urgent. The bare statistics of increasing poverty and wider inequalities are stark enough, but they do not take account of the most iniquitous aspects of the Thatcher regime. They give insufficient weight to the deliberate attack made by the Tory Government on the disadvantaged, and the moral climate which that has engendered.

The catalogue of iniquity is a long and depressing one. It ranges from the deliberate use of high unemployment, with its disproportionate effect on the disadvantaged, to the cuts made in the services on which the unemployed depend. It includes the deliberate attempt to force low-paid and unskilled people into the labour market at still lower wages, by cutting the benefits they receive and removing the minimal protections – such as wages councils – they could turn to when at work. It embraces the redistribution of the tax burden in favour of the rich and the use of macro-economic measures such as the over-valuation of the currency, which increases the value of assets but destroys the jobs of wage-earners.

These policies have done real damage to the lives of many people. Those whose life chances have been permanently blighted – by the closing of educational opportunities, or by lack of training, or by lack of employment as school leavers or in middle age, or because untreated illness has disabled them – are, however, those whose voices are least likely to be heard, and who have also been silenced by the propaganda efforts made by the Government to convince them and others that they are to blame for their own difficulties. It has always been one of the least attractive features of those who wield power that they succeed in putting the blame for their failures on their victims, who are often so demoralised that they believe it.

The moral stance which holds that the weak and powerless are blameworthy finds its reflection in the view that the successful are not only morally superior, but are entitled by virtue of their success and moral superiority to ignore the needs of those less fortunate. This moral position also mirrors an electoral calculation. Mrs Thatcher and her Government have concluded that they need pay no attention, in electoral terms, to the least advantaged third of the population. Their interests can be attacked and their moral claims repudiated with impunity, and without threatening the appeal the Tories have been able to make to the more prosperous.

Mrs Thatcher has, in other words, persuaded many ordinary people to make common cause with the rich and powerful, and to create a sort of alliance against the weak and disadvantaged. This is very much in the interests of the privileged, who will willingly share a small part of their privilege with others if the prize is that their privilege is not only not seriously challenged, but is also encouraged to grow. The consequence is that the class structure of our society, and the importance of privilege and inequality, has been greatly reinforced.

This cynical approach does, of course, create great problems for the Labour Party. We have no option but to defend the interests of the disadvantaged, but we are then easily portrayed by the Tories as exclusively concerned with a failing and undeserving minority, and therefore out of sympathy with the relatively successful majority. The creation of a social and moral climate in which the successful recognise society's responsibilities towards the less privileged is a prime task for socialists in the next decade.

ECONOMIC FAILURE

The Thatcherite legacy is not only one of social and moral damage. It also involves substantial failures on the economic and industrial front, which will have to be made good if we are to face our future with any confidence.

It would, of course, be churlish not to welcome the improvements in our economy in the latter part of the decade, whatever qualifications might then have to be introduced. The fall in unemployment owes something, it is true, to the manipulation of the statistics, but the rise in living standards is real enough, as is the growth in national output. The contrast with the grim days of monetarist-inspired recession in the early 1980s is clear.

This guarded welcome need not, however, induce us to accept the Government propaganda about an economic miracle; nor need we listen too attentively to businessmen who assure us, on the basis of anecdotal evidence, that, because high unemployment and quiescent trade unions have made the job of management easier, we have somehow resolved all our economic problems.

The facts are against such an easy assumption. The first point to make is that the recent improvement, while welcome, has done little more in most respects than restore us to the position we were in when the present Government came to power. It is as though the Government threw the economy over a precipice in 1979 and is now congratulating itself as we inch our way back up the cliff-face to the point at which we started.

Manufacturing output, for example, has only just recovered its 1979 level, after languishing well below it throughout the 1980s. This persistent shortfall has cost the nation billions of pounds in lost national wealth. Manufacturing investment is still below its 1979 level, and for much of the period has fallen worryingly short of the minimum required even to maintain the capital stock.

Two-thirds of the more than a million jobs that have been lost since 1979 have been in manufacturing – a much sharper rate of loss than can be explained by long-term trends. Our trade performance in manufactured goods has been disastrous. A surplus of £8 billion in 1979 (in today's prices) has been transformed into a deficit of more than £14 billion in 1988. This turn-round of £22 billion in our manufactured trade may be 'neither here nor there' according to the Chancellor, but if that volume of goods were still being produced in British factories, it would be worth more than one and a half million jobs.

These items must certainly be entered in the debit column in assessing this Government's economic record. But surely, Government supporters claim, there are major items on the credit side as well?

Let us try to judge this according to the Government's own claims. They claim to have reduced the tax burden so as to provide increased incentives to hard work and enterprise. The truth is that the tax burden – for the country as a whole and for the overwhelming majority of families – has been higher throughout their term of office than it was in 1979. Moreover, even if they had succeeded, there is no evidence that reducing the tax burden would have made any difference. The Treasury-financed Brown Report failed to detect any incentive effect from tax cuts.

The Government claim to have cut public spending so as to release resources for the allegedly more productive private sector. The truth is that, while North Sea oil revenues, asset sales and buoyant revenues from the consumer boom have enabled them to eliminate public borrowing, public spending as a proportion of national wealth has been higher throughout the greater part of their term of office than it was when they came to power, while the recent slight reduction, far from freeing resources for the private sector, has been accompanied by excessively high interest rates designed to reduce demand. Indeed, even the fiscal surplus of which the Chancellor boasts cannot be used for fear of the inflation and balance of payments consequences.

The Government claim to have been able to reduce inflation by a strict application of monetary discipline. The truth is that the monetarist policies in whose name so much damage was inflicted have been quietly abandoned; if £M3 were really the sole determinant of the inflation rate, as the monetarists claimed it to be, we should now have inflation of over 20 per cent. The money supply has in fact grown very rapidly, fuelled not by the much-maligned public spending, but by a record explosion of personal and private credit.

But surely, it will be said, inflation has come down? Yes, but not in response to anything the Government has done. British inflation today is higher in proportion to that of other industrial countries than it was in 1979, and is now the highest of all the advanced industrial countries. To the extent that it has been lower in absolute terms than it was in the 1970s, this has mainly been in response to world commodity prices, and not because of the now-abandoned monetarism.

On one thing, however, ministers and businessmen are agreed. Whatever pain we have been through, the prize has been worth it – British industry is at least leaner and fitter and more competitive. This claim is repeated *ad nauseam* by ministers and is enthusiastically endorsed by businessmen. Yet the truth is otherwise. Every one of the indices of competitiveness that are customarily used – from relative export prices to relative normalised unit labour costs – shows that British industry is less competitive today than it was in 1979, and that it has been so throughout the 1980s. What would otherwise be the mystery of our deteriorating trade performance is therefore unravelled.

If the facts are so much against the Government, why are they widely regarded as having managed the economy so successfully? One answer is that they have succeeded in keeping a large number of people happy, even though the economy as a whole has been doing badly. Another answer lies in three words – North Sea oil.

The oil has certainly raised living standards for the majority, transformed the Government's own finances and, for a time, relieved us of our perennial balance of payments constraint. What did not happen, however, was the use of North Sea oil resources to regenerate the British economy. On the contrary, the oil's impact seems to have been literally counter-productive. The Government says that it was inevitable that North Sea oil would displace part of our manufacturing capacity; yet this did not happen in Norway, where oil was proportionately much more important to their economy and where they managed to maintain high levels of manufacturing output, investment and employment.

The Government also defends itself by saying that North Sea oil resources are now represented by much-increased assets abroad. These assets may produce a *rentier* income for some sections of the population, but they have done very little to strengthen the productive capacity of the British economy, and they are in any case now diminishing rapidly as our productive weakness manifests itself in a balance of payments deficit that has to be financed.

The fact is that North Sea oil has come and largely gone, and we are no better prepared to meet international competition than we were a decade ago. The real case to be made against the Government on their management of the economy rests not so much on past failures as on their failure to show any concern for our economic future.

The consumer boom over which they presided was enjoyable as long as it lasted, but it was always unsustainable. There has never been any particular magic required to live beyond our means for a brief period; the catch has always been to grow fast and achieve full employment without running into balance of payments and inflation problems. Our present situation, in which we still have 2 million unemployed, and even then face rising inflation and a truly alarming trade deficit, is therefore not a very great achievement. Boosting demand has always been the easy bit; it is on the supply side that the Government has failed so miserably.

The next decade, with the single European market and newly industrialising countries entering the field, will belong to those countries that most successfully embrace the new technology and improve the skills of their workforce. It is here that the present Government's failures will count against us most severely. We spend less on Research and Development than other comparable countries, and a higher proportion of what we do spend goes on relatively unproductive defence R & D. We are neglecting basic science. We have the worst-trained work-force in the advanced industrial world. Manufacturing investment in new plant and equipment is lower than is needed even to sustain the present stock. Our industrial infrastructure is crumbling. And the oil will no longer be there in such volume to sustain us.

The boom was unsustainable because it was unbalanced. It was unbalanced between consumption and investment and between imports and exports. It was unbalanced between those in work and those unemployed. It was unbalanced in the priority that continues to be given to the interests of the City rather than to those of manufacturing. Above all, it was unbalanced between one region and another. A boom which hardly touched the real economies of the depressed regions had to be brought to an end because of over-heating in the South-East. The higher interest rates designed to slow down a rampant consumer boom in the South-East helped to snuff out any potential growth in the manufacturing economy on which the regions depend. And all the time, through measures like the immense differential increase in purchasing power represented by tax cuts for the rich and social security cuts for the poor, the regional bias was intensified.

The case against Mrs Thatcher is this – that after the pain of monetarism, after the sacrifices made by millions of unemployed, after the assault on public spending and the Welfare State, after the tax cuts for the rich and the harsh treatment of the poor, after the unparalleled opportunity of North Sea oil, we are essentially back where we started, with inflation rising and higher than in competitor countries, with unemployment still twice as high as when she started, with a balance of payments crisis looming, with our industry losing markets, and having made no provision for the more competitive world which faces us in the 1990s.

It is the failure to prepare the British economy for that more intense competition which is the most serious charge. We face 1992 with many declarations of airy optimism from the Government, and a great deal of expenditure on glossy television advertising, but with virtually no detailed preparation for the assault that will be made on our market by powerful competitors. We shall, on present form, pay a heavy price for the lack of concern the present Government has shown for our economic future. So much for the economic miracle.

THE POWER OF INTERNATIONAL CAPITAL

Finance capital and democratic governments have been engaged in a long struggle over many years for control of the central aspects of economic policy. The battle goes largely unnoticed by the public and commentators, and at times is virtually uncontested by government. Right-wing governments, which see themselves as in any case representing the interests of capital, are not inclined to contest capital's view of matters; while governments of the Left are often too unsure of themselves and too easily cowed by the power of capital to give much of an account of themselves.

The struggle is nevertheless of crucial importance, and the last ten years have seen the balance of advantage swing decisively in favour of finance. Monetarism was, after all, no more than a complete capitulation by Government to the money markets; and even now that its heyday has passed, we are still told by Mrs Thatcher that 'you can't buck the markets'. Financial orthodoxy continues to dominate economic policy-making. The consequence has been a substantial loss of democratic control.

Capital, generally represented by the bankers and the financial institutions, has always argued that some economic questions – usually to do with the value of money, and therefore involving questions of exchange rate and monetary policy – are too important to be left to the whims and vagaries of democratic politics. According to this view, the electoral pressures on politicians in democratic countries will always tempt them to try to provide more than can really be produced; they will therefore take risks with the value of money by, amongst other things, printing money, encouraging inflation and thereby depreciating the currency. Decisions on these matters must accordingly be removed from the hands of politicians, and entrusted to the more cautious and responsible care of the bankers.

This is a profoundly anti-democratic view: its acceptance would mean the removal from the hands of democratically elected governments of the decisions that really matter. It is also profoundly unconvincing, since it offers no satisfactory explanation of the puzzle that, while the creation of credit by governments is said to be dangerous, the creation by the banks of private credit (usually devoted to consumption and asset inflation rather than investment, and taking place on a much greater scale and subject to much less control) is perfectly acceptable.

Despite these objections, the bankers' view has had remarkable success. The bankers have been adept at inventing controls and targets – whether the Gold Standard, the exchange rate or the money supply – and at persuading governments that they matter. Once caught by the bankers' leash, governments discover that giving absolute priority to a given monetary target means that all other aspects of policy have to be subordinated to that target; and since the target is always within the control of the money markets and is therefore extremely sensitive to their confidence, or lack of it, in Government policy, the consequence is that the bankers are able to control the central aspects of Government policy merely by withholding approval where they think it appropriate.

British governments of all persuasions have been peculiarly susceptible to this tactic. Sometimes that susceptibility has been overt and deliberate, as in the case of the Gold Standard or monetarism. At other times it has been reluctant and less obvious, as in the case of the pressure put on Labour governments by threats of sterling crises and losses of confidence.

It is against this background that we must view the political pressure to accept and endorse the internationalisation of capital. Capital has always been more or less free to move across national boundaries, and to that extent it has always had the opportunity of escaping national political control. It is only with the post-war drive towards free trade, the development of global capital markets and the advent of major international groupings such as the EEC, however, that the real possibilities of this escape from political control have become apparent.

Right-wing governments, anxious to see policies of financial orthodoxy entrenched, and content to hand over control of policy to central banks, nevertheless fear the advent of left-wing governments, which might not be so content. The internationalisation of capital offers the chance of entrenching monetary policy in the hands, not just of national central banks, but of central banks organised internationally – well beyond the control, not to say second thoughts, of potentially recalcitrant and radical politicians.

The advent of a single European market, based on the free movement of capital, goods and labour, and therefore hostile to intervention by Government, has also contributed to the creation of a Europe fit for multinationals, in which they can operate without fear of interference by national governments. It is no accident that Mrs Thatcher endorsed and helped to create the single European market, and now opposes the establishment of any countervailing political authority.

The impetus given through the Thatcher years to the power of finance at home and of international capital and business abroad confronts the Left with a very real problem, to which our reaction has so far been very uncertain. On the one hand, we have recognised the difficulty, if not futility, of trying to resist the internationalisation of capital and industry. On the other hand, we have been far from clear as to whether it is possible or desirable to impose conditions on this development, and, if so, what form those conditions should take.

It is important to establish two principles, in the hope that, however difficult they may be to act upon in practice, we have at least some idea of what is our desired outcome. First, the organisation of capital should not be allowed to outstrip the political organisation needed to control it. The absence of an appropriate political control, whether at the national or international level, should be good reason for resisting the internationalisation of capital.

Secondly, a commensurate political organisation should be accepted as appropriate only when it in turn serves the requirements of democracy. This is particularly important when it is suggested that the solution to the problem of keeping track of international capital is to organise politically on a matching international scale. This is perfectly acceptable, and is indeed the right response, as long as the consequence is not that Government as well as capital escapes democratic control.

There is, in other words, a danger that international capital will be in a position of such power that it can compel politics to be re-formed in its image and to suit its purposes. Unless we are very careful, Government will be forced to abandon the level of operation that is best suited to its democratic purposes and to operate instead at the international level, which suits the multinationals and international capital, with the result that Government is actually captured more thoroughly on the international scale than was ever possible on the national scale.

This danger follows from the important truth that democracy

is not just about elections and the elective principle. We can have as many elections as we wish, but we still do not have democracy unless those elected and the institutions to which they are elected carry out the functions of Government that the people they claim to represent wish them to carry out. The fact that the European Parliament is elected, for example, does not of itself mean that it acquires democratic legitimacy; for that to happen, people would have to consent to being governed by a body organised on a Europe-wide basis. Without that consent, elections are hardly relevant to the question of democracy. It is doubtful, to say the least, whether there is yet – in Britain at least – that sense of belonging to a Europe-wide civil society that would legitimise this form of Europe-wide Government.

This means that the solution to the problem of bringing international capital under political control does not necessarily lie in creating political institutions on the same international scale, if those political institutions do not command the democratic allegiance of the people they claim to represent. Indeed, such a solution would simply exacerbate the problem, by adding to the loss of control implicit in the internationalisation of capital the loss of democratic political representation as well.

The exercise of control at the international level, to the exclusion of national governments, may well mean, in other words, that international capital simply escapes effective control, since it is then able to deal with an international bureaucracy which necessarily lacks democratic legitimacy and which serves mainly as a buffer against the proper attempts of national governments to protect their electorates. Yet if we insist on attempting to exercise control exclusively at the national level, then international capital (and its industrial and commercial equivalents – the multinationals) will find it easy to play one national Government off against another, constantly bidding down the controls individual governments may wish to exercise. What, then, is the answer?

Some form of political control organised on an international basis must, of course, be put in place to restrain the power of international capital, but that power must be democratically accountable to institutions in which the people have confidence and to which they naturally relate. What this means is that we should concentrate on co-operation between governments, each accountable to its own electorate, rather than on the transfer of power from governments to international institutions. Governments themselves must organise the necessary controls and agree the means by which they are enforced. Co-operative arrangements, harmonised standards, the full exchange of information and constant monitoring are the keys to the effective control of the multinationals.

The creation of a centralised European Government is, in other words, not necessarily the answer and may actually make the problems worse. There are, of course, many functions that were once appropriate to the nation state but are now more easily and effectively dealt with at the international level: the control of pollution, co-ordinated economic management and co-operative arrangements in high technology or large-scale industrial development are obvious examples. The proper control of international capital has to be handled with special care, however; and the Left must be careful not to be hustled into an inappropriate response.

## THE REINFORCEMENT OF PRIVILEGE

The economy as a whole may have performed badly under Mrs Thatcher; it may be in a weaker and less competitive position, and less able to provide the basis for national advance in the 1990s. For some people, however, the Thatcher years have meant personal aggrandisement and advance, because Thatcherite policies have deliberately shifted the balance of power in favour of the already powerful.

The mechanisms are all too familiar. Power has been concentrated in the hands of the rich and powerful by measures such as the income tax cuts for the top income groups, the relaxation of capital taxation and the introduction of the poll tax. The beneficiaries of these measures are exactly the same people who have benefited from the substantial rise in pre-tax salaries at the top end of the scale and from the great increase in corporate profitability.

But it has been more than a matter of regressive tax changes and income rises. One of the most powerful factors in removing power from the disadvantaged and transferring it to the already privileged has been the huge increase in the value of assets, and in particular of property, that has flowed from the economic policies, which have generated such a high degree of asset inflation.

This has been of special significance to those who own their own houses. They have seen a huge increase in the value of the most important asset they own, which has not been matched by any comparable increase in the wealth or income of non-home owners.

Because this has benefited what is probably a majority, since two-thirds of households are now owner-occupiers, it is easy to conclude that it cannot represent an increase in privilege. The fact that the privilege is widely shared, however, does not reduce its significance; if anything, it makes the position of those who have been left out even less tolerable – both in actual material terms and also in the political sense that they are less likely to command any sympathy or remedial action from what is in effect a privileged majority.

It is often argued that the rise in the value of houses has not meant a real increase in the resources and wealth of owner-occupiers, since the gains they make when they sell are counter-balanced by the higher prices they have to pay when they buy. This is only partly true, and is likely to become progressively less so. The rapid increase in house prices has first of all acted as a disincentive to others – first-time buyers – who wish to enter the housing market, and to that extent has provided a buffer to owner-occupiers against the erosion of their privilege; and it cannot in any case be argued that owner-occupiers as a whole have not become substantially wealthier in relation to the rest of the population.

The ease with which the increased equity can be converted into other and more liquid forms of wealth, and the increasingly important extent to which people inherit the increased wealth that accrues to their owner-occupying parents, have to be taken into account. The most important point, however, is that the huge rise in the value of housing is not new wealth; it has to come from somewhere, and it must, by definition, come from those who are not owner-occupiers. This redistribution has

occurred through an asset inflation which has dispro-
portionately raised the value of a particular range of assets and at
the same time devalued in comparative terms the wealth and
income of others.

The decisive shift in favour of the wealthy has not just been a
matter of tax changes and benefits to certain categories of
asset-holders. It has also been brought about in non-economic
ways, by measures that have enlarged the freedom of action of
the wealthy but restricted the powers of the less privileged.

The prime example of restrictive measures has, of course,
been the diminution in trade union rights, but this has been
backed up by reductions in employment rights and attacks
upon the income levels, benefits, services and choices available
to low-income people. Those organisations, like local authorities, that have particular responsibilities for the services on
which the disadvantaged are likely to depend have been special
targets.

At the same time, the choices available to the wealthy have
been greatly widened. This has been an important consequence
of the various forms that privatisation has taken; the more the
provision of services like education and health care is entrusted
to the market, the more the wealthy are able to make their
advantage in the market-place count.

The privatisation process has produced other and even more
obvious benefits to a privileged class. It is certainly true that the
extension of share ownership (to whose popularity the sale of
privatisation issues at a substantial discount certainly contributed a great deal) benefited a large number of people,
including many employees of the privatised enterprises; but
this sweetener was a relatively small price to pay for the huge
increase in wealth which privatisation meant for a much smaller
group.

Those who derived the real benefits were the City institutions
that earned huge fee incomes from privatisation flotations and
the commercial concerns – as in the case of the British
Aerospace purchase of Rover and the Royal Ordnance Factories – that acquired valuable assets from the taxpayer at
knock-down prices.

Whereas pensioners and other dependents on the State's
support have found their claims to benefit subjected to careful

scrutiny, and working people's organisations have been rigorously regulated, what is remarkable about the beneficiaries of the Government's generosity in privatisation is the absence of any real control over or regulation of their activities. The City remains regulated, not by a statutory body but by the Securities and Investments Board – a private company limited by guarantee. Breaches of City rules are rarely followed by effective sanctions. The attitude still seems to be that City fraud is not really crime.

A striking instance of the absence of effective regulation is the whole field of takeovers and mergers. This has been of immense importance, not only as an area where the fate of billions of pounds' worth of assets has been decided, but also as a major means of concentrating power and reinforcing the already excessive centralisation of British industry, while providing a huge fee income to City institutions. It is also fair to say that, while takeovers and mergers provide enormous benefits to a small minority, numerous academic studies have found they add nothing to the general welfare, and may even be positively harmful to the economy as a whole.

The most striking feature of this activity, however, is that – unlike trade union activity, for example – it is substantially free of effective regulation. It can hardly be claimed that the subject is too insignificant to warrant regulation, yet the rules governing takeovers and mergers are largely voluntary – a Takeover Code administered by a voluntary Takeover Panel – and even breaches of statutory law in this field are ineffectively investigated and punished.

The virtually unique openness of and ease of access to the British market for corporate control, by comparison with the tightly structured and controlled markets elsewhere, might be thought to call for a robust interventionist policy from the Government. Yet the Tory Government has deliberately refrained from any such intervention, thus ensuring that the public interest and the interests of the workers (whose jobs are usually the first victims of a takeover and who – in the absence of any rights to consultation – are usually the last to know what is happening) are ignored, and that the powerful are able to increase their stranglehold over the national economy.

## THE NEW TECHNOLOGY

There is a further sense in which the modern industrial economy threatens to increase the concentration of power in the hands of those who control capital. The increasingly capital-intensive nature of much modern economic activity has meant that the importance of capital in relation to wealth-creation is growing steadily, with a corresponding diminution in the importance of labour. The new technology on which competitive production increasingly depends is not only very often expensive – and therefore available only to those with access to capital – but it also displaces, and is intended to displace, labour.

This feature of the modern industrial economy has had particular significance in Britain under the Tories – a political significance as well as an industrial and economic significance. In other advanced industrial countries, investment in new technology has been more or less politically neutral. There, while new technology has certainly strengthened the position of capital, it has been seen primarily as a means of increasing output rather than reducing the need for labour; the new capital equipment has not been intended to replace labour, and the contribution that labour makes to that increased output has remained important. Indeed, in some ways, the value of labour has risen in line with the new technology, as new skills are both required and acquired.

In Britain, on the other hand, much of the investment in new technology has been, either explicitly or implicitly, not so much for the purpose of increasing output as of replacing labour; it has been directed quite deliberately at altering the balance of power between capital and labour – and in particular organised labour. There are too many owners and managers who see new machines, not as the path towards greater productivity and competitiveness, but as the instrument of a political victory over a recalcitrant workforce. That is an important part of the explanation of an apparent paradox – that manufacturing productivity has improved sharply at the same time as our manufacturing trade and competitiveness has declined. What has happened is that in those parts of British industry that have survived, new investment has improved productivity, but the investment has not been sufficient to maintain and improve capacity across the board.

The British failure to provide adequate training in new skills is a further manifestation of this attitude – and, unfortunately, an all too typical example of the way in which class and economic conflict in this country is so often allowed to take precedence over the national interest. A management that is fearful of its privileges and doubtful of its abilities would prefer to see the workforce unskilled and unemployed, rather than see everyone share the bigger cake that new technology could provide.

If new technology is sometimes seen in this country as a weapon in the class struggle, it is, of course, a double-edged sword. New technology, once developed, is often inexpensive to use and produce and, in the hands of individuals and small groups, can help to increase their power in relation to others who are intrinsically more powerful. This can be true both of producers, where access to an inexpensive new technology can enable an effective challenge to be made to existing power concentrations, and of consumers, who should be able to use new technology such as inter-active cabling to improve their information about and access to the market, so as to make it work better for them and improve their position in relation to powerful producers. The question of whose interests will be served by the new technology is one of the most important challenges facing socialists in the 1990s.

THE CONCENTRATION OF POWER IN THE MEDIA

The Press and the broadcasting media are a case in point. The Thatcher years have seen a dangerous and growing concentration of ownership – which is not only objectionable in principle but also reinforces in practical terms the support a right-wing Government can expect to receive from subservient media.

Information in modern society is power; information technology is the field in which technological advance most obviously impacts on daily lives; and information technology – the satellites, the computers, the cabling – is expensive to develop and is largely a monopoly of big business. What this means is that the great flood of information on which modern society increasingly depends, to which the ordinary citizen is increasingly exposed and which increasingly forms opinion and creates the context of political debate, is controlled by a handful of major corporations – not to say individuals – whose views and values it naturally reflects.

These views and values are naturally those of the Right. With the obvious exception of Robert Maxwell, the nature of current media ownership, dominated as it is by powerful individuals and business tycoons, inevitably means that the individual values reflected are those of the successful businessman. The Left already suffers from the constant presentation of issues with a right-wing bias; the problem can only intensify as business tightens its grip on media whose influence will become all-pervasive in the 1990s.

On the other hand, the new technology offers, at least in theory, a means of escape from this trap. Once established, the new technology of electronic communications and broadcasting is relatively cheap and easy to use, and access to it, again in theory, should be increasingly available to a wide range of people. It ought, therefore, to encourage the sort of small-scale, multifarious, pluralistic media that are the exact antithesis of a concentration of power we might otherwise fear. Easy access to and a wide spread of production facilities ought to guarantee a range of heterodox opinion and values that would protect against brainwashing and the projection of a single capital-oriented view of society.

Which of these two possible developments will prevail will depend very much on the political will, preferences and sensitivity to the issues of the Government of the day. Here, in other words, is a major area of political conflict, where the socialist approach will produce a very different outcome from that which will result if the dangers are not foreseen and averted.

Without intervention by Government, it is a fair bet that the power of capital, based on its existing position of strength and near-monopoly, will succeed in overcoming the tendency towards proliferation that might otherwise be induced by the cheapness and availability of the new technology. It is so much in the interests of the existing giants to use their current market power to exclude newcomers – and that current power is so overwhelming – that it will require a determined effort by Government to wrest that power from them. Only a socialist Government, committed to plurality and the diffusion of power, will be adequate to the task.

The problem is already acute. Three companies sell over 70 per cent of all daily national newspapers and over 80 per cent of the national Sundays in Britain. This degree of concentration restricts consumer choice and places enormous power in those few hands – the power to decide what is news, to set the political agenda, and to hire and fire editors.

The problem goes beyond mere newspaper ownership. Rupert Murdoch, for example, has a powerful interest in newspaper distribution through his subsidiary TNT. He has world-wide newspaper and publishing interests, including, and in particular, the highly significant stakes in Reuters, the *Financial Times* and the *South China Morning Post*, which are primarily concerned with financial information.

He has production facilities in film and television, and in newspapers world-wide. He is taking a dominant position in satellite television. He will soon be able to beam Murdoch-controlled news into millions of homes around the globe. Other companies are following suit.

The UK dimension of the problem is likely to grow, as the Tory Government presses ahead with deregulation. This is sure to mean, paradoxically, an even tighter grip for those already entrenched in positions of power. The commercial stakes will become so high that only a handful will be able to afford to play, and length of purse – and the willingness to take losses – will increasingly decide who survives.

Nor has the hoped-for ease of access promised by the new technology materialised. Ironically, it was a pioneer of the new technology and the exemplar of the little man – Eddie Shah and his *Today* newspaper – that recently fell victim to Rupert Murdoch. The episode also graphically illustrated the ineffectiveness of the current laws governing monopoly in newspapers. The special rules designed to safeguard the public interest were contemptuously brushed aside by Murdoch, just as he had done in the earlier case of *The Times*. In both cases, the rules were ignored by a complacent Government which continues to swap favours with News International.

This is in marked contrast to the position overseas, where strict rules govern the concentration of Press ownership. News International was itself forced to divest by the American Federal Communications Commission (FCC) rules; the French have recently demonstrated the force of their rules in the case of the Financial Times bid for *Les Echos*. In Germany and Sweden equally tough rules apply. In many cases the restrictions include requirements as to the nationality of ownership (Murdoch was compelled to become an American citizen) and control the extent to which newspaper ownership is compatible with interests in the broadcasting media.

The case for a more effective regime to prevent and dismantle an undue concentration of ownership is overwhelming. To act on that case would not of itself produce a more diverse and freer Press, but it would be a major step towards that objective. It would also provide safeguards against future trends that are already visible and are extremely alarming.

THE ASSAULT ON FREEDOM

It was Lord Hailsham who warned against the perils of an 'elective dictatorship'. It is perhaps ironic that it is under a Government of which he was a member – and a Government allegedly dedicated to the primacy of the individual and in particular to the concept of individual rights and freedoms – that the threat of an 'elective dictatorship' has taken its most dangerous form in modern times.

Mrs Thatcher has presided over a Government formed increasingly in her own image – bossy, domineering, narrow and arrogant in personal terms, and authoritarian, illiberal, centralising and intolerant of opposition in terms of action and policy. The *Index of Censorship* published in 1988 was only one of the growing expressions of concern at the erosion of civil liberties in Britain.

It is not necessary to over-state the case – Britain remains by most standards one of the most truly free countries on earth. But the trend is unmistakable. While the rich and powerful may feel themselves more free to pursue their own self-interest, without let or hindrance from the Thatcherite State, British society as a whole has been forced to become more subservient to the State's interests, and more sensitive to the State's displeasure in a whole range of activities.

The present Government has, first, pursued a relentless course towards greater centralisation. This is particularly evident in its treatment of local government, which has found its financial independence virtually terminated, its powers severely curtailed and transferred to central Government, and its reputation gravely damaged by a sustained propaganda campaign against it. In some obvious instances, as in the case of the GLC and the metropolitan counties, the attack has taken the form of outright abolition and the suspension of elections – and all this at a time when a growing and worrying regional imbalance has given greater force to the case for the devolution of power to the nations and regions of the United Kingdom.

This assault on local government has, however, simply been one aspect of the Government's general attack on institutions it regards as hostile. Thus, the trade unions have been substantially handicapped by the statutory removal of legal immunities and powers, and in the case of the workforce at GCHQ trade union membership has actually been outlawed. The trade unions have generally been treated as hostile and un-British and have been effectively excluded from participation in the nation's affairs.

Other institutions have also felt the heat of Government hostility. The University Grants Commission was replaced, for example, by a body working directly to the Secretary of State – just one instance of the way in which central Government has arrogated power to itself in the field of education. The Training Commission was abolished altogether when the TUC refused to co-operate with the Government's training scheme.

The broadcasting media in particular have been bullied and browbeaten. The BBC has been subjected to a long campaign by Government ministers alleging bias, laxity and disloyalty. No one can doubt that such a campaign has its effect, not so much on programmes that are obviously censored (though there has been no shortage of those) as on programmes that are not made or are made differently, or in news bulletins that soften items unfavourable to the Government and give prominence to those that flatter it.

The IBA, too, has had its reverses, and has felt the effect of threats to its independence. The establishment of the Broadcasting Complaints Council, the threat to public service broadcasting implicit in the establishment of, but thankfully not carried out by, the Peacock Commission and the further dangers arising from the deregulation of broadcasting have all created an atmosphere of challenge to the freedom of the broadcasters.

The Press, too, has had its share of difficulties. The Press in this country is too often a watchdog which does not bark. It is quick to probe the foibles and peccadillos of individuals, but less keen to challenge the Government. This is largely because the popular Press in particular, as we have seen, is in the hands of a dangerously concentrated ownership, which is voluntarily subservient to Government because it shares the Government's attitudes and prejudices.

A large part of the Press has willingly played its part in identifying the Government's enemies – the trade unions, social security claimants, ethnic minorities, foreigners – and creating hostility against them. For its part in this dangerously incestuous relationship, the Government has expressed its gratitude through the award of knighthoods to helpful editors and by setting aside, as in the case of *The Times* and *Today*, the rules meant to deter the concentration of ownership; but it has also repaid the Press by claiming the right to censor reports that are not to its liking.

Perhaps the most notorious of these attempts, because the most long drawn out and least successful, was the protracted litigation over the *Spycatcher* affair; there have, however, been many other cases, such as those involving Sarah Tisdall, Clive Ponting and Lonrho, which have been equally illustrative of the Government's attitude towards the release of information. A particularly telling incident was that involving the expulsion of the Cuban ambassador in 1988; such information as was vouchsafed to the British public about this was obtained, not from the Government of a supposedly free democracy, but from the authorities in a Communist dictatorship.

The Tory Government has had no hesitation in using the Official Secrets Act 1911, the Contempt of Court Act 1981 and the Police and Criminal Evidence Act 1984 to restrict the flow of information to the public, to gag journalists, and to compel them to reveal their sources. The Official Secrets Act of 1989 seems certain to perpetuate and extend these constraints. We are still a long way from the Freedom of Information Act that is needed if citizens are to be properly informed about the actions of Government.

The most worrying aspect of this restrictive attitude has been the assumption that the interests of the State and of the Government are identical. Both the judiciary and the Press, to their shame and in contradiction of their true role, have at times succumbed to this dangerous view.

The Government has reinforced its attitude towards dissent by ruthlessly using its powers of patronage. Government appointments have been increasingly made on a political basis; the answer to the question 'Is he one of us?' has increasingly determined the acceptability of candidates for public positions. Political opponents have been removed from office, in bodies ranging from health authorities to boards of school governors. The Civil Service has been increasingly politicised, with promotion made obviously conditional on political acceptability and withheld from those who do not comply. Again, it is not just the overt instances that matter, but also the general effect they have on attitudes and behaviour, setting new and dangerous norms.

Hand in hand with this attack on institutions seen to be hostile to the Government has been the assault on individual values of which the Government disapproves. The enactment of Section 28 of the Local Government Act 1988 was the classic sign of a Government prepared to use its legislative powers to dictate what people should think about essentially private matters of sexual behaviour and morals.

Underlying this whole area is the Government's constant denigration of those who do not conform. The attempts at censorship, the attacks on the living standards of the poor and the constant emphasis on self-help have reduced the power, freedom, self-confidence and self-esteem of those who do not match the Government's concepts of success.

How is it that a Government apparently committed, in all its public statements, to the rule of law and to individual freedom should have been responsible for such a dismal catalogue of mean and repressive measures and attitudes? The answer is that it flows, perhaps surprisingly, from the Government's ideological stance.

The modern Tory Party is fundamentally opposed to what it calls 'the Nanny State' – the State whose function it is to provide guarantees to individuals that, whatever their individual circumstances, certain minimum standards will be met. According to this view, the State has no reason to do what individuals can in principle do for themselves. Whether or not those things get done is not the responsibility of society but of each individual; it is only through the exercise of that individual responsibility that freedom is maintained. The Tory belief, owing much to Nozick and Hayek, is that the State should disengage; it is for each individual to work out his or her own salvation.

The argument that the individual's freedom is maximised by the withdrawal of the State may look strong – even if it is, and is admitted to be, a freedom to succeed or fail, and even though those who fail will inevitably suffer a significant diminution of freedom. In other senses, however, the minimalist State favoured by the Tories is an extremely powerful, centralised and authoritarian one, requiring, as the price of the freedom of some to succeed, a substantial degree of conformity from the rest.

This is because, in ensuring that the individual is not inhibited in the quest for self-advancement by the claims of others, the State necessarily finds itself obliged to provide a buffer for the rich and powerful against those claims. This inevitably means that the State plays more than a purely neutral or negative role in striking and maintaining a balance between different individuals in society. It finds itself, as part of its function of resisting – in the name of individual freedom – the social claims of the less successful, enlisted in positively serving and protecting the interests of the successful.

By merely appearing to hold the ring, therefore, the Thatcherite State in effect commits itself to the existing distribution of power and privilege. The defence of those interests imposes the need to maintain a politically rigged status quo, which in turn necessitates a considerable investment of State power. Stability, hierarchy, respect for authority become important preoccupations.

This is not all. The minimalist State, deliberately non-interventionist and therefore claiming little power of its own, can fulfil its function of defending the status quo only by aligning itself with and utilising the power of the already powerful. Without their support, the State could not perform its functions. The interests of the powerful and of the State become identical.

Such a State inevitably finds itself dedicated to the suppression of dissent and the promotion of conformity. The State that is self-consciously detached from questions of social justice, or making good the deficiencies of the market, or diffusing power, nevertheless finds itself wholly committed to defending its own interests and – by definition – those of the powerful. It is, in fact, a highly interventionist State, but one which intervenes – concentratedly and therefore powerfully – across a narrow range of issues and in a narrow range of interests. Its preoccupations are with security, secrecy and the maintenance of authority.

This is the explanation of the paradox that a Tory Party which proclaims its commitment to freedom has proved itself so authoritarian in Government. The consequence is that, for many people in society, freedom is not only reduced by the disadvantage they suffer in relation to the powerful, but is also constrained by the need to conform to the dictates of a State apparatus that reinforces their disadvantage and cuts off their means of escape.

It is therefore an important part of the socialist project to prise open the Tory State's grip on those who claim the right to dissent, or who do not succeed in Tory terms, or who challenge the powerful in various ways. This can be done only by substituting for the dismissive attitude of that State towards the weak, and its incestuous relationship with the powerful, a doctrine that proclaims the equal rights of every member of society simply by virtue of citizenship and espouses the concept of the State as the servant of all the people rather than as the protector of privilege.


EXCESSIVE CENTRALISATION

The problem of matching political institutions to appropriate functions does not arise only in the international sphere to which we referred earlier. Whether because governmental functions are, as a simple matter of efficiency, more easily carried out at a local or regional level or because people feel it easier to relate to political institutions which are less remote, there is a powerful case in modern and complex societies for administering and providing services as close to people as possible.

Particularly in a highly centralised state like the United Kingdom, we could certainly make gains, in terms of both efficiency and democracy, by devolving power downwards and sideways. Yet the Thatcher record is one of growing and dangerous centralisation, as the consequence of the assault on local government, the opposition to devolution, the concentration of economic power in the South-East and the virtual abandonment of regional policy.

The growing regional imbalance, which has gathered pace under Mrs Thatcher, is both economically and politically wasteful and dangerous. It threatens the political cohesion of the State, it jeopardises a uniform and sustainable economic advance, and it is an affront to social justice, democracy and the diffusion of power. The socialist response should be a conscious attempt at decentralising both government power – through the establishment of a new level of regional authorities – and economic power, through the encouragement of a new regional infrastructure of financial institutions, centres of research and further education, and industrial investment.

The increasing complexity of Government means that it should not be surprising that some functions should be suited to the level of international co-operation, some to the nation State and yet others to regional or local government. Socialists should concern themselves with what might be called the need for appropriate Government – the notion that Government functions should not be lumped together and carried out by only one tier of Government, but should be consciously analysed and allocated to the institutions that are best placed to meet the needs of efficiency and democracy.

This is naturally a preoccupation of the Left rather than the Right; a function of Government exercised at an inappropriate level will mean a loss of democratic control, because power held and exercised inappropriately is power granted unnecessarily.

The absence of proper democratic control will usually mean that power is exercised not only inappropriately, but very often autocratically, by those who already exercise considerable power.

This is of little concern to the Right. The concentration of power is something they welcome and encourage rather than resist. The Right will always instinctively favour the exercise of political power at the highest possible level, as an expression of their belief that power is not to be diffused but should be the prerogative of an already powerful élite.

The growing importance of these issues provides a major opportunity for the Left. For as long as the nation State represented the highest and most extensive level at which political power could be exercised, because that was also the scale on which capital was naturally organised, the Right could identify itself with the nation State. There was no incompatibility between their allegiance to capital and their allegiance to the State. They were able to exploit the one in pursuit of the other.

Now that capital is no longer organised on a national basis, the Right is compelled to abandon its traditional exploitation of patriotism for political ends. Capital now demands an international structure; it has no patience with the political structures to which most ordinary people feel allegiance. This means that not only the State, but also the region and locality, are no longer available to the Right as vehicles for advancing their political interests. The Right can no longer be the patriots.

The Left, on the other hand, is the natural heir to these potent political attitudes. In the name of democracy, accountability and the diffusion of power – in the name, in other words, of socialism and in opposition to the hijacking of political power by remote and powerful people – we are now the natural representatives of that powerful sense of community which most people feel, and of the connection they naturally perceive between the community they instinctively relate to and the exercise of political power.

## THATCHERITE BLIND SPOTS

The sins of ten years of Tory Government have not only been those of commission. An aggressively right-wing ideology has also meant that many major issues have been neglected or, at best, have commanded only a lip service delivered in the interests of political expediency.

Foremost among these issues has been the growing recognition of the importance of the role of women in society. It is at first sight surprising that the country's first woman Prime Minister should be open to the charge that she has shown little interest in the rights and role of women. Yet it is not as surprising as it seems. Mrs Thatcher has taken a deliberately anti-feminist stance, on the basis that, if she can reach the top, there can be no real obstacles to the advancement of women. She has, it is true, exploited her femininity, but she has done so quite consciously for the purpose of succeeding in what she accepts as a 'man's world', in which masculine values and attitudes are the norm.

That is why the Tory record in such matters is so poor. Women's rights at work have been reduced, not extended. We lag shamefully behind in the provision of child care and other facilities to enable women to play their full part in the national economy and in the support of themselves and their families. We fail to train women in the new skills that will be so important in the coming decades.

It is not, however, just as economic agents that women have been neglected by the Tory Government. The social importance of women and the contribution they can make has also been undervalued; the role of women as the focal point of social units, as mothers and carers, as the cement which holds society together, as the manifestation of an alternative and perhaps superior range of social values has also been overlooked.

This neglect of the role of women constitutes a real challenge to the Left. We must not only address the practical policy questions – of improving, for example, training and child care facilities; we must also re-think our attitudes to feminist issues. We must be ready to recognise that feminism should not be regarded only as a statement of demands on behalf of women, but as an agenda which illuminates the whole range of political and social issues, whether directly or exclusively affecting women or not. Above all, if we expect to be taken seriously in these matters, we must show our awareness of their importance in the way we conduct our own affairs and in the role which women play in them.

Similar points can be made in respect of other forms of discrimination, whether on the basis of race, religion or sexual preference. The Right insists on conformity; the Left – on the basis of a socialist recognition of the importance of each individual – will offer a genuine respect for individual difference. We must accept that the best judges of the effects of discrimination and of the means by which it should be counter-acted are the victims themselves, and at the same time recognise that discrimination inevitably imposes a social and economic cost on society as a whole.

Concern for the environment is another issue which makes only a belated and unconvincing appearance on the Thatcherite agenda. Mrs Thatcher has begun to pay attention to the environment because her political intelligence tells her that there is a rising level of concern about the issue. It is not, however, an issue that sits comfortably with her underlying political philosophy. It is hard to reconcile the common interest in the long-term environment with the primacy accorded in Tory philosophy to the drive for personal and material gain. That is why, again, the record is such a poor one – why Britain remains the 'dirty man' of Europe, continuing to discharge raw sewage on to our beaches and to drench the rest of Europe in acid rain.

Socialists should be quick to argue that a concern for the environment can be given practical effect only if the community's interest can be effectively identified and organised, and supported by the political will to enable it to take precedence over individual concerns which are inevitably narrower and more short-term. Those who want to see this happen may not recognise it as socialism; but without becoming too preoccupied with labels, we should not hesitate to claim the essentially socialist nature of what an effective concern for the environment will mean.

# CHAPTER THREE

## *The Socialist Response*

### GROUNDS FOR HOPE

As the Labour Party confronts our recent disappointments and the challenges for the future, what resources can we draw upon to equip ourselves for effective Government and electoral success in the 1990s? What does or could socialism mean in modern Britain? How do we remain true to a recognisably socialist body of principle and values, and at the same time match the aspirations of a prosperous and technologically advanced society?

As we have seen, the experience of the last two or three decades has been a dispiriting one for the Left, and for the Labour Party in particular. Given all the factors – international, historical, intellectual, sociological, accidental, personal – that have combined to throw us on to the defensive, it is perhaps remarkable that the Labour Party has survived as well as it has, that it remains the only viable alternative to the Right and that it is still a major contender for power. This stands as a testament to the robustness of the principles and values we stand for, and to the unease of many people concerning the social division and lack of compassion for the disadvantaged over which the Tories have presided.

We should also take courage from the fact that, even in the adversity of the Thatcher years, we have been able to develop at least the rudiments of a counter-strategy. This is particularly true in respect of our growing interest in decentralisation. The long years of Thatcherism have at least taught us that we cannot always rely on exercising power from the centre and that strategies are needed to protect and develop more localised interests, wherever this may be possible. Hence, the useful pioneering work done by local authorities and enterprise boards on developing local and regional enterprise, and the growing interest in decentralised forms of common ownership. We can make these ideas grow.

There is also a message of hope from developments abroad. Socialist governments have guided the fortunes of some of the most successful countries in the world – Sweden and Austria come to mind – and provide a beacon light for the Labour Party in Britain. Gorbachev's reforms in the Soviet Union have not only transformed the prospects for European co-operation and disarmament, but also show how a political force of the Left can modernise itself and face the future.

Even in those countries that retain right-wing governments, there has been a subtle change of mood. This is partly a consequence of the swing of the fashion pendulum, as the inevitable and cumulative failures of Government are now deposited in the debit account of the Right, but, more important, it is a response to the stock market crash of 1987. Even right-wing governments learnt the lesson then that markets could not be trusted to get things right.

The blind faith in the judgment of the market has now given way to a more sober appreciation of the market's arbitrariness and capriciousness. The belief that 'you can't buck the market' may still be enunciated by Margaret Thatcher, but it is contradicted by her Chancellor, who now pursues policies of the most calculated intervention in matters of interest rates and exchange rates. The monetarist domination of economic policy by the monthly vagaries of the money markets or the foreign exchange markets, over which even Denis Healey reluctantly presided, is now a thing of the past.

Just as the cession of this centrally important territory to the free market in the 1970s had the ratchet effect of leading to further concessions to the market in other areas of policy, so the reclaiming of economic policy from the free market will mean that the ratchet will work in the opposite direction. If the market cannot be trusted in the central areas of economic policy, why should we trust it (without at least some attempt at supervision and regulation) to produce the right answers elsewhere?

There is also now much less disposition to believe that the Tory medicine has worked in economic terms. There were many people in Britain who were prepared to strike a sort of

Faustian bargain with the Tories. They disliked the harsher aspects of Tory social policies and they worried about the moral climate; but they agreed to put up with these less acceptable aspects of Tory Government for as long as Mrs Thatcher delivered rising living standards to them and their families individually and apparent economic success to the country as a whole.

The realisation that the Tories are no longer able to keep their side of the bargain, that the much-vaunted economic success was no more than a profligate and breakneck consumption of the once-for-all bonus of North Sea oil, and that all the old problems have now re-emerged in an even more acute form, have all led to a growing repudiation of the bargain. The social disunity and the moral harshness which were once accepted as a perhaps necessary price for economic success now have a higher profile and command a less willing acceptance when economic success is no longer delivered.

Mrs Thatcher herself is aware of this so far subterranean shift in sentiment. She recognises – presumably because her pollsters tell her so – that she and her Government are now operating at the far reaches of political dogma. There is not one person in a hundred thousand who, if asked a year or two ago what the Government should be doing in 1989, with a 100-seat majority and three years to run, would have replied 'privatising water and electricity'. Mrs Thatcher is forced to acknowledge that, in pursuing these measures, she is no longer operating entirely in the mainstream of opinion.

It is for this reason that she is now trying to develop an agenda that is not of her own choosing. When she talks of her concern for the environment, or for the inner cities, these are not her issues; they are issues that naturally arise on the Left's agenda but that she feels compelled to deal with because electoral considerations demand it. This shift in the political agenda should be of great encouragement to the Left.

All of this means that the long post-Crosland decline of the Left may be coming to an end. The chance is now there for the Labour Party in Britain to learn from the more successful experience of socialists abroad and from our own painful domestic experience, to take advantage of the change in intellectual climate and in the perception of political and economic factors which is now becoming apparent, and to reflect that concern for social justice and cohesion which has proved so remarkably impervious to the temporary hegemony of the Right.


## A SOCIALISM FOR THE 1990S

It is nevertheless fair to say that British socialism has lost its way in recent years. The electoral reverses, the declining class support and the apparent invalidation of the Crosland analysis have left us dangerously vulnerable. Those who, from the fringes of the sectarian Left, offer to step into the breach with various Marxist or Trotskyite prescriptions have succeeded only in making matters worse, by increasing the widening gap between Labour and its natural supporters.

Socialism in this country has never had a strong ideological base. Crosland identified a number of contributors to its tangled skein – the Lockeian philosophy of natural law, Robert Owen's emphasis on co-operation rather than competition, the pre-Marxist labour theory of value, Christian socialism, Marxism, the theory of rent as an unearned increment, William Morris and anti-commercialism, Fabian gradualism, the Independent Labour Party's (ILP) general concern for 'the bottom dog', Welfare State paternalism, syndicalism and guild socialism, the doctrine of planning – and even this list, to which must in any case be added the sort of vague labourism that has long underpinned the Labour Party, is by no means exhaustive.

What stands out is the variety and heterogeneity of this list of antecedents and the impossibility of ascribing to any one doctrine the status of engravings on tablets of stone. What has to be said, however, is that British socialism pre-dates and has wider concerns than the capitalism of any particular time or place.

It is, of course, natural that capitalism should be the major preoccupation of socialists in modern society, since capitalism is the prevailing economic and social order and represents the concentration of power, which, as I shall argue, is the antithesis of a socialist society. But socialism must be more than an adjunct of capitalism. Socialists must have something to offer if and when capitalism, defying Marx's supposed laws, evolves and transmutes into something different – the sort of post-capitalist society that we seem to be approaching in the Western world at the end of the twentiety century.

Socialism is, in my view, a body of principles and social aims that will be relevant and, with necessary adjustments, applicable in any society. It is a mistake to believe that society will somehow reach some final stage of evolution, and will then settle into a permanent and changeless condition. Society will always evolve; the challenges faced by socialists will always be renewed; there will never be a moment when we can say that socialism has been achieved and there is no more for us to do.

We are therefore obliged constantly to review and renew our socialism, asking whether our basic principles call for a new or revised application in modern conditions and how they are prepared to meet new challenges. We do not have the luxury of imagining that the world stands still. If we insist on maintaining that socialism can be brought about only in certain forms and in a pre-ordained order of succession, we cannot complain if society chooses to evolve in a different way from that predicted and therefore concludes that socialism no longer has any relevance.

We are also obliged to translate our basic principles into practical politics. The electorate will want to know, particularly from a Party which is self-consciously ideological in approach, what we stand for by way of fundamental beliefs; but they will also want to know how those principles will be applied when it comes to the hard practical issues of current politics. Will they mean more jobs, better services, cleaner streets, fatter pay packets?

If we want to earn the support of the electorate in the 1990s, we have to offer a socialism that expresses the instinctive attachment of the British people to the social virtues of justice and compassion, one that offers them encouragement in the quest for higher standards and greater choice, freedom and autonomy, and that also demonstrates a clear appreciation of what is required to achieve economic success as we turn the century. This requires a great deal of new thinking, but our starting point must be the principles, values and attitudes that made us socialists in the first place.

THE DIFFUSION OF POWER

What, then, are the basic socialist principles to which we should adhere but whose application we should constantly review? Whatever differences there may be in analysis and prescription, most socialist writers and thinkers seem to stand for some basic values – equality, solidarity, co-operation, social concern, collective responsibility. Can we go further than that? Can we say what it is that underpins these values, so that we can apply them to new and changing circumstances?

I argued in *Socialism and Freedom* that what unites and gives cohesion to these attitudes and provides an underpinning to socialist thought is a basic response to a universal social phenomenon. That phenomenon is the natural tendency of all social organisations to distribute power unequally, and in most cases to concentrate power in a few hands. In all societies, those who are stronger, cleverer, richer, luckier will acquire power at the expense of others in society, and will then use that increased power to entrench their privileged positions.

The response to this natural and inevitable phenomenon is one of the central questions to which politics addresses itself. In some societies, the naked assertion of power will prevail; but in democratic societies, some response to the concentration of power will be offered by those contending for support. It is in the making of that response that socialists make their distinctive contribution.

The conservative or paternalist response is to accept that such a concentration of power inevitably occurs, to point out that it brings with it certain advantages – such as placing power in the hands of those they consider best fitted to use it – and to find ways of mitigating the effects of its unfairness so that those without power are reconciled to its loss. Thus, great emphasis is placed on the virtues of stability and hierarchy, and on respect for authority; those with power recognise that they owe paternalist responsibilities to the less powerful, without, of course, being willing fundamentally to challenge the basic distribution of power.

The *laissez-faire*, or liberal, response is very different. (This approach, incidentally, is closer to Thatcherism than to what is traditionally regarded as conservatism.) Here, the concentration of power is not only acknowledged, but is positively welcomed and encouraged as the pre-condition of human and social advance. No attempt is made to mitigate the unfairnesses that are accepted as the price necessarily paid for that advance. In any case, it is argued, everyone – even the least advantaged – will eventually benefit from the advances made possible by concentrating power in the hands of the most able.

A further response, which has often characterised politicians of the Centre, is what might be described as the equality of opportunity response. According to this view (which Tawney castigated as the 'tadpole philosophy'), there is little to be done to prevent the concentration of power, and much to be said for it; its unfairness, however, is to be mitigated by ensuring that everyone starts off as nearly as possible in a position of equality. If, after that, natural advantages or luck should mean that some should obtain much more power than others, then so be it; we can at least then be fairly sure that they deserve it, while those less fortunate can at least hope to benefit from the general social advances which the powerful bring about. There is something of this view (although, to be fair, he introduces some important modifications, including the requirement that inequality must benefit the least advantaged) in the work of Rawls.

What marks out the socialist is that he or she alone responds to the concentration of power by consciously trying to do more than mitigate it. The socialist response is positively to counteract and inhibit the concentration of power by putting in place institutions and mechanisms that remove power from the hands of those who would normally accumulate it, or that prevent it from getting there in the first place. The socialist is therefore someone whose objective is the diffusion, rather than the concentration, of power; it is in the interests of that diffusion – and in the interests of the ordinary and comparatively powerless citizen – that the socialist will challenge the power of the capitalist, or the landlord, or the employer.

The socialist makes the case for the diffusion of power on two grounds – both ethical and practical. A socialist diffusion of power is required, first, in the interests of the moral worth and personal fulfilment of each individual, but it is also important to the cohesion and practical effectiveness of society, which can only benefit from a proper distribution of power and can only suffer if power is accumulated in the hands of a few.

If the central question of politics is the distribution of power, and if the socialist is someone who wants to see the widest possible dispersal of power in a given society, a number of important consequences flow. The socialist challenge to the capitalist is not made simply because of the accumulation of capital and the power that brings with it; it is made because, in modern society, capital is one of the prime sources of power, and a system that allows a minority to control and accumulate capital to the exclusion of others is one that inevitably creates great concentrations and inequalities of power.

Contrary to Marx, however, the socialist still has something important and central to say of societies where capitalism has not developed or has been in some way modified. The socialist will be concerned about concentrations of power, whatever form of power may be involved and whatever principles are used to determine its distribution. Thus, as well as challenging concentrations of economic power, the socialist will also resist the concentration of political power, and will see political democracy as an integral part of the socialist project of diffusing power.

Even in economic terms, the socialist will be alert to respond to all forms of concentration of power, and not just to that in the hands of the capitalist. He or she will wish to restrict the power claimed by the bureaucrat or marketing man, the trade union official or employer. In any given society, whatever its characteristics, the socialist will always resist the powerful in the interests of the greatest diffusion of power that is possible.

Since the most effective diffusion is secured by an equal distribution of power, the socialist will always be committed to equality. An equal distribution of power (always bearing in mind Tawney's dictum that equality does not mean identity) will in turn mean that the greatest possible power should be exercised by each individual in society. This is what gives the lie to the constant charge from our political opponents that socialism is destructive of the interests of the individual. On the contrary, only socialists are concerned with the rights and interests of every individual, from the least to the most powerful; only the socialist understands that true individual freedom is to be secured only through the equal distribution of power; and only the socialist knows that freedom in society is to be measured by the freedom available to the least free.

I have argued elsewhere that the power we should be concerned with is the power to make real choices and that this rests on the distribution of social and economic power in society – the 'primary goods' with which Rawls is concerned. I would argue, however, that Rawls is wrong to distinguish between liberty (which he says must be distributed equally) and other primary goods (which he says should be distributed according to his principles of equality of opportunity and benefit to the least advantaged). In my contention, the concepts of individual liberty and the exercise of social and economic power are inseparable.

An unequal distribution of social and economic power will inevitably affect freedom. A comparative shortfall in access to decent health care, housing, education or other basic aspects of modern life will circumscribe choice to such a degree as to make nonsense of any notion of the equal distribution of freedom, for what is freedom if it is not the power to make choices? An unequal distribution of these primary goods (however high the absolute standards may be) will also lead to a loss of individual self-esteem, which Rawls characterises as the most important primary good, and which, he says, must be distributed in such a way as to benefit the least advantaged.

For the socialist, therefore, and for anyone else concerned about individual freedom, there is no conflict or incompatibility between greater equality in the distribution of basic social and economic power in society and the maximisation of individual freedom; they are actually one and the same thing. Those who concentrate on the freedom a given (and usually powerful) individual might claim, while paying no regard to the effect which that individual's claim to an unequal share of social and economic power might have on the freedom of others, have no more than a travesty of a true concern for individual freedom. If each individual in society is to be as free as is possible, given the claims of others to an equal freedom, that can be achieved only by an equal distribution of freedom, and that in turn depends on an equal distribution of the social and economic power which enables real choice to be made.

THE POWER TO CHOOSE

It is one of the clichés of modern politics – and one of the most
damaging to the Labour Party – that we cannot make up our
mind what we stand for. As with all clichés, it both suggests and
masks the truth. The truth is that ten years out of office, and
fifteen years away from the last time our programme was
endorsed by the electorate, we have naturally suffered some loss
of confidence; and, without power, we have not had the chance
to develop our thinking against both the stimulus and the
discipline of having to confront real problems.

That loss of confidence has at times meant a paralysis of
uncertainty as to whether to go forwards or back. We have
found it particularly difficult to respond to the changes in
people's expectations that have occurred during the 1980s.
Should we reject them as essentially Thatcherite, and risk being
condemned as hopelessly out of touch? Or should we accommodate them and adapt them to our purposes, and be lambasted in
some quarters as traitors to socialism?

The first step towards escaping this confusion and uncertainty is to disentangle those changes that are desirable and
inevitable, such as greater prosperity and choice, from those –
irresponsibility, selfishness and greed – that we oppose and that
properly distinguish us from our opponents. In recognising and
endorsing those changes we find welcome, we do not concede to
Thatcherism. Instead, we escape the burden of attacking what
is, after all, both popular and acceptable, and can give much
greater point to the issues on which we have something
distinctive, important and socialist to say.

Nowhere is this more true than on the question of individual
choice. This is an issue which the Tories have made very much
their own. Tory propaganda has constantly emphasised their
zeal in extending, through measures like council house sales
and privatisation, the choices apparently available to ordinary
people.

We have quite properly responded by pointing out that the
choice apparently created by Tory policies has been an illusion
for most people, that it has been cynically used as a cloak for
increasing privilege, and that it is simply inadequate as a means
of meeting the nation's need for quality services and essential
strategic investment.

Too often, however, these critical arguments have become subsumed in what appears to be a general hostility to greater individual choice. At the very least, we have seemed unwilling to recognise that greater prosperity means that people are less likely to accept – in fields like housing, education and health care – an imposed provision which was appropriate to a past era but is now inadequate to meet the new demands for greater flexibility and choice.

We have insisted that there are only two options – that if we reject a market provision that will inevitably be prejudiced against the disadvantaged, there is no alternative but a collective provision which tells people what they must have. This polarised view leads us apparently to deny the greater choice which many people rightly welcome and seek; and it cuts us off from a line of argument and policy that would allow us to show that socialism alone can deliver real choice.

We have, for example, paid too little attention to the possibility that, within the security provided by collective provision, a much greater range of choice could and should be provided. The NHS is the best guarantor of proper health care for all, but why shouldn't women be able to choose a woman doctor if they so wish? In publicly provided housing, why shouldn't people be able to choose the form of tenure that suits them best?

What we should be saying is that greater choice is to be welcomed, and that there is no way we should wish to frustrate its development or turn the clock back. We should say that not only is greater choice entirely consistent with our principles, it is also an important socialist aim – an essential consequence and concomitant of the rising prosperity we seek.

But we should also say that while greater choice is welcome, merely making choice available is not enough. If that is all that happens, those able to exercise choice will scoop the pool at the expense of those less privileged. By substituting the market for collective provision, the Tories have arguably extended the mechanisms of choice, but they have failed to ensure that these increased opportunities are not limited to and exploited by a privileged minority. Indeed, in many of their policies, the Tories have made it more difficult for many people to compete for market provision.

If choice is to be made real and substantial in the lives of

everyone, what matters is the practical power of each individual
to choose. A choice does not exist unless it can be exercised.
Choice is denied in all those cases where people are prevented –
by lack of income, health, education, information, leisure –
from exercising the power to choose. Extending the mechanisms of choice without acting to overcome these disabilities, as
the Tories have done, is actually to limit choice for many,
because it increases their comparative powerlessness in the face
of the increased real choice available to the already powerful.

The concept of choice is therefore inseparable from questions
of power and freedom. Choice can be widened and made real for
everyone only if power is diffused and shared. That means – in
the case of collective provision – greater accountability and
democratic control, and a greater attention to building the
mechanisms of choice into the structures of provision.

Where market provision is the preferred alternative, this
requires a conscious effort to empower and enable each citizen
so that market power is fairly distributed and choice becomes a
practical reality rather than a chimera. This effort cannot be
undertaken individually but requires society to take a hand.
Only society as a whole has the resources, the vision and the
responsibility to the wider interest to ensure that each individual, simply by virtue of citizenship, has the power to make
real choices.

That must be the socialist message for the 1990s. The
emphasis on greater individual choice in the 1980s was in many
ways welcome and necessary for those fortunate enough to
benefit from it – but it was too supportive of existing
inequalities and privileges, too disabling and exclusive of so
many who lack the power to choose, to be a true agent of
liberation or a sound basis for social cohesion and national
success.

We do not need to go on contesting the 1980s. We can now
move the argument forward, looking to the issues that will be
relevant in the 1990s. The British people, having been fed the
rhetoric of choice and having seen the mechanisms of choice
extended so that those with the power to choose have benefited,
will now want some real choice for themselves. They will want
something better for the 1990s. That something better is a
modern socialism which offers not just the traditional socialist

virtues of compassion, tolerance and social justice, but also a recognition that individual freedom and national advance depend on extending to everyone – through social action – the power to choose.


## THE IMPORTANCE OF SOCIETY

The commitment to individual freedom and equality flows from the socialist concern for the diffusion of power, but also from the socialist appreciation of the importance of society and the individual's relationship with it. If society is regarded as no more than a random agglomeration of individuals, there can be no structure to validate, confer and deliver an equality of power, and therefore of freedom, to each individual. The socialist, again uniquely, recognises that individual freedom – for every individual – depends upon founding the rights of that individual in his or her membership of society.

In her notorious remark that 'there is no such thing as society', Mrs Thatcher has unerringly identified the central difference between her own political vision and that of the socialists she has sworn to eliminate from British politics. Here, in one succinct phrase, is the Thatcherite glorification of the individual – of individual effort, responsibility and success – and the repudiation of the socialist insistence that it is society that makes individual success possible and that guarantees individual freedom.

In the Thatcher view, each individual exists as an atomised, fragmented entity, making contact with other individuals only in opposition to or competition with them or by accident or painful necessity. The responsibility of each individual is entirely to him or herself (or, by extension, to dependants) and is fulfilled only by striving to improve the individual lot, even at the expense of others. If others benefit from the efforts of one individual, that is a welcome but essentially peripheral by-product of the central activity and duty – the advancement of the individual interest.

In this view, there is no place for collective effort or collective responsibility. No duty is owed by one individual to another or by society to the individual or by the individual to society.

There is no benefit to be gained, either individually or collectively, from recognising common cause with others.

There is, it is true, room for compassion – as a specific *ad hominem* and *ad hoc* response to the plight of another – but there is no need for individuals to join with others to organise a common, general and continuing response to the needs of others. Indeed, such an effort would be futile and counter-productive. It would mislead the disadvantaged into believing that their salvation lay in the efforts of others and divert them from making the necessary effort on their own account; and it would distract the successful from the best contribution they can make to the welfare of others, which is to pursue their own self-interest.

To the extent that society has any function, it is, according to this view, that of setting up a 'night watchman' State, whose responsibilities are limited to defence against external aggression and the maintenance of law and order so that property rights and other rules designed to enable the individual to pursue his self-interest are enforced. This minimal State nevertheless demands and commands the allegiance of each individual, on the basis that the State alone can ensure the individual's right to strive for his or her own advantage and to preserve it when acquired.

Paradoxically, as we have seen, the minimal State is also an extremely authoritarian State. It exists to maintain the existing order and, by necessary implication, to serve the interests of the powerful; those who challenge the powerful will also be deemed to challenge the State and will accordingly attract the State's censure and punishment.

How well has this Thatcherite vision served this country? Apologists for Thatcherism claim that the 'enterprise culture' brought about by the new drive for individual achievement, and the liberation from the dead hand of 'welfarism', has revolutionised this country's economic performance and prospects. As I have already pointed out, this view is sustained by little more than the anecdotal evidence of those who have personally benefited from the greater inequality brought about by these policies.

But while the beneficiaries are naturally very appreciative of Thatcherite priorities, for many others, and for society as a whole, they have been a source of weakness, disunity and bitterness. This is partly because making the rich richer and the poor poorer is an affront to the British sense of fair play, but it is also a common-sense response to a very evident social malaise, in which the cohesion of society and the wide acceptance of common moral values are clearly breaking down.

Thatcherites are hardly in a position to complain or even to express surprise at this consequence of applying their precepts. If it is every man for himself, and self-regarding attitudes are lauded and rewarded, it is not surprising that the force of moral principles should diminish, since morality is essentially an other-regarding set of rules and principles and is entirely displaced if self-interest is accepted as the over-riding imperative.

This lack of morality may be just about tolerable in general society when manifested by the rich and powerful – not because greed, selfishness and ruthlessness are in any sense less reprehensible when they take the form of City fraud or tax evasion, but because the rich and powerful are often able to camouflage their moral deficiencies in the applause and deference which greets their material success. It is found to be less acceptable, however, when manifested by the disadvantaged, for whom there is less camouflage available and yet for whom the imperatives of Thatcherite selfishness are just as compelling, if not more so. The Thatcherite reaction to their attempts at self-help and at coming to terms with the loss of what Rawls calls the most important primary good – self-esteem – is a good deal less admiring, because those attempts are seen as challenging the status quo which allows the powerful to prosper.

Little wonder, then, that some disadvantaged groups should attempt to set up their own self-sufficient set of Thatcherite attitudes. Young hooligans and vandals are a case in point. One of the reasons they have proved immune to society's revulsion and vilification is that they know that society, and particularly the successful, regard them as losers, whether hooligans or not; the only way they can achieve some self-esteem is by having the confidence to set their own standards. As a result, the only opinions that matter to them are those of their peers. Outrage on the part of outsiders is merely confirmation that their behaviour has a value that is independent of, and a challenge to, the standards of the rest of society.

It is, in other words, an inevitable consequence of the Thatcherite denial of society that that denial should take different forms – and forms that are displeasing to the very people who believe they have most to gain from the denial. If we are told that the only game in town is winner takes all, with no holds barred, we cannot complain if some of the losers choose to play by their own rules. That is why there is a growing undercurrent of violence in our cities, declining respect for the law, an almost tangible crumbling of the social cement that holds us together.

It seems that the Government have belatedly recognised the corrosive effects of their policies and precepts – or perhaps, more pointedly, the electoral risks that accompany the rising concern about these fundamental issues. We are told that the concept of the 'active citizen' will make good the deficiencies; but how effective can the individual citizen be without social organisation? If we are to rely on entirely commendable but nevertheless capricious and unreliable acts of individual generosity and voluntary effort, how can that spasmodic and marginal response possibly meet the scale of society's needs?

And which individuals are likely to respond to the plea that they should be 'active citizens'? Surely not the reviled losers, who are not only exhorted to play a game they cannot win, but are told on top of this that their failures are their own fault and that it is no good looking to society for help and support. The only individuals who might volunteer to be 'active citizens' are those who have a vested interest in the status quo – and their deliberately individual efforts, whether as Lady Bountiful, vigilante or censor, are hardly likely to reconcile the disaffected to their fate.

The dilemma for the Government is that the only effective way of countering social disintegration is to begin the task of re-building society – and to do so on the declared basis that society has a value, the very proposition that Mrs Thatcher denies. This is the great opportunity for socialists to seize, since we, more than any others, base our political philosophy on the principle that the individual needs society in order to flourish.

We must put forward the argument that it is social co-operation and organisation that makes human advance possible. None of us, however talented or exceptional, could conceivably achieve or enjoy even a fraction of our material, cultural or intellectual attainments if it were not for the fact that we live in society. Society's well-being is, of course, dependent on the contributions made by numberless individuals; but none of those contributions would even be possible, let alone count for much, if calculated as individual accretions to the sum total, without the collective and cumulative benefits of living in society.

That over-riding fact should be the most important determinant of our relations with each other and with society as a whole. It should mean that none of us has a greater claim than others to the benefits that living in society affords. If our individual contributions, however great they may seem to us (and however important they may rightly be to each of us individually), are of only the most marginal importance by comparison with the great fact of social co-operation, they can form no basis for a grossly unequal claim by some to society's benefits. Even the individual who lays claim to no more, as he sees it, than he himself has created, is overlooking the fact that even that apparently quantifiable benefit owes almost everything to the context created by society as a whole.

There is, in other words, a status conferred upon us by the mere fact of our belonging to society. It is our participation in the great joint enterprise that should determine our relations with each other as individuals and in society, and it is this status, which does not vary from one individual to another, that should determine the distribution of rights and power.

There is here the basis of a theory of citizenship, a status acquired quite automatically, which defines the minimum rights each of us can rely upon and which can be used to protect our individuality. Here, too, is a protection for the ordinary citizen against the overweening power of the State – a power which, paradoxically, is encouraged by theories supposedly dedicated to the supremacy of the individual but whose practical effect is to allow the State to dominate all but the most powerful individuals.

There is another sense in which the concept of citizenship, or of an equal status derived naturally from being in society, actually promotes rather than devalues the worth of the individual. This is a strictly utilitarian argument, and it rests on the perception that if it is the collective and cumulative effort of society that is by far the most important determinant of our well-being (at least in the public sense, as opposed to issues of personal happiness and fulfilment), then it follows that we should concern ourselves with the contributions potentially available from each one of us, and not rely solely upon the contributions made by the most talented or powerful or fortunate.

If each individual is regarded as an important contribution to the well-being of society (simply because the collective effort necessarily and massively outweighs the value of any individual contribution, however great), then each individual is given a proper value by society. It is in society's interests and in the interests therefore of each member of society that each individual should fulfil his or her potential, and that society should make the investment – in education, health care, decent housing – to make that possible. This is the true doctrine of individualism – one that gives importance to each individual, not just to the minority who grab an unfair share of power by depriving and exploiting others.

There is, therefore, both an ethical and a utilitarian basis to the socialist concern for equality and social justice. This is the answer to Mrs Thatcher's blinkered and arid denial of society. This is the means by which we can heal both the bruised self-esteem of the individual and the wounds of society, and restore that sense of social cohesion, justice and unity which is the essential mark of a successful society.

LOOKING FORWARD

This, then, is the theoretical basis on which socialists should approach the practical questions of modern politics. These are the basic socialist values and principles – individual liberty, equality, citizenship, the diffusion of power, the importance of social and collective action – which should be given practical application when we are faced with the issues of the 1990s, and which will produce the policies to deal with them.

These principles may not have the satisfying certainty of Marxist analysis, nor may they constitute quite the same stirring call to arms as one based on class warfare. But they are a proper expression of the socialist opposition to injustice, repression and exploitation, and of the socialist concern for the welfare and value of each human being, for social justice and for social harmony.

They produce in practical terms a very different socialism from the one our opponents delight in attacking. There is here nothing of the images of centralised power, the authoritarianism, the bureaucracy, the defence of vested interests, the indifference to individual aspirations, the unwillingness to accept change or to innovate, which we have at times allowed ourselves to be saddled with, and which have provided such tempting targets for our enemies.

Instead, we derive from these principles a socialism that, in practical terms, will mean policies for decentralisation, pluralism, greater individual rights, and higher public and private standards, as well as greater social justice, freedom and equality. We can have confidence that such a socialism will make a potent appeal to the electorate and will provide a truly socialist basis for effective and beneficial Government.

# CHAPTER FOUR

# Socialism and Wealth Creation

## ATTITUDES TO SUCCESS

Socialists have always, in their varying ways, been concerned with those who are disadvantaged. They have taken up the cudgels on behalf of the exploited workers, or have espoused collectivism and co-operation as the means by which social responsibility can be exercised on behalf of the less fortunate, or have felt a broad commitment, as G.D.H. Cole put it, to the 'bottom dog'.

In modern terms, or in the terms that I suggest, the objective of diffusing power has necessarily meant that an increase in power for the less powerful and a corresponding reduction in power for the most powerful are essential aspects of socialist policy. There is no way in which socialists can abandon that commitment to the under-privileged and that objective of a greater equality of power – and there is no one else in politics who will undertake the defence of those interests.

This central theme of the socialist approach does, however, impose special responsibilities and special difficulties. On the one hand, there is no point in making the commitment to the defence of the weak, if we are never in a position to put that defence in place. In a democratic society, where the political power to change things is acquired by enlisting the support of the majority, the defence of the weak (who are, in today's society, a minority) can be made only by engaging the support of the strong.

Socialists have been at times reluctant to acknowledge this. It is almost as though an appeal to the strong is seen as a betrayal of the weak – as though dealing with the strong carries with it a moral taint, which sullies the purity of the commitment to the weak.

This curious view, which still informs a powerful current of opinion in today's Labour Party, has allowed a Thatcherite attack which has been electorally and politically damaging to us. The attack has taken the form of propagating the message that 'winners vote Tory, losers vote Labour'. The message is a potent one; it suggests to those who feel they have succeeded (even modestly) that part of their success is a change in their political attitudes and voting habits – that voting Labour is the mark of those who have failed.

The Thatcherite message has, of course, helped them towards this view, not only by welcoming them to the ranks of the successful, but also by assuring them they need feel no concern for those they have left behind. But we have ourselves aided this perception, by appearing to berate those who succeed as class traitors and moral lepers, and by seeming to try to frustrate (in matters like home ownership) their achievement of what they see as success. It is not so much that these people have forgone their earlier allegiance to the Labour Party as that the Labour Party has rejected them.

The consequence is that, while the Labour Party has been very good at making speeches and passing resolutions about our anxiety on behalf of the weak and disadvantaged, we have cut ourselves off from the political support and power which alone can turn our protestations into effective action. We are limited to standing on the sidelines, wringing our hands, while those whose interests we want to defend are left to the tender mercies of Mrs Thatcher.

If we are to escape from this Thatcherite trap, we have to rethink our attitudes towards success. We have to make it clear that success in their own terms does not debar people from voting Labour and supporting the socialist cause, and that, on the contrary, the success they seek is better achieved through socialist politics and is the objective of socialist policies.

We have to say that we welcome the success they seek, that we want to be part of it, to encourage it, to make further success possible, and, indeed, that much of it could not have happened if it were not for reforms brought about by Labour govern-ments. But we should also say that the success people seek must mean more than being able to buy the latest video-recorder; it must also mean the sense of living in a successful community – a community that is happy with itself, that has a sense of unity and cohesion, and that is not riven by conflict and disfigured by gross inequalities.

This issue is related to another, which also causes difficulties for the Labour Party – the question of how to deal with the drive for material advance. There is much in socialist values that, by correctly emphasising the worth of ethical, environmental and social considerations, would oppose the glorification of material consumption. This attitude is given additional impetus by our proper scorn for the exclusive capitalist preoccupation with material gain.

An acceptance that there is much more to life than higher and higher material consumption does not necessarily imply, however, that socialists should oppose the objectives of economic growth, efficiency and prosperity. It is the elevation of these objectives to the exclusion of all others that is objectionable; but their achievement is an important part of the socialist project. It is not incompatible with other socialist objectives, and can, indeed, be considered a necessary pre-condition of achieving those, such as a higher level of public spending, that require additional material resources. Even objectives such as a cleaner environment are more effectively achieved through greater efficiency.

Socialists should not be inhibited, therefore, from addressing the aims of greater wealth creation. Indeed, any hesitation on this score can easily be portrayed, in Crosland's terms, as the middle class 'pulling up the ladder behind them'. Our concern for the economic welfare of the majority and the need to diffuse economic power more widely should also predispose us towards encouraging growth and prosperity.

Economic failure is, after all, not necessarily against the interests of, or particularly painful to, the powerful and dominant, who are still able to use their power to ensure that they suffer no appreciable absolute loss; indeed, the extent of their privilege is increased in comparison with the real losses suffered by the victims of failure.

It is, in other words, the least privileged who have the greatest interest in economic success. They have the most to lose from economic failure, particularly in comparison with others in society, and, because they have the most ground to make up, the most to gain from success. Socialists have little chance of appealing for their support or truly representing their interests if we do not recognise their aspirations for higher material standards, in terms of their own personal consumption and choices as well as in terms of the better public services brought by greater wealth.

Nor should we distinguish between economic success for the country as a whole and personal prosperity for individuals. The two are inextricably bound up together and should be endorsed equally by socialists. As I shall argue later, we must not be so mesmerised by the importance of the collective interest that we denigrate the validity of individual aspiration, nor should we overlook the fact that the only way in which economic success, or any other benefit, can be delivered effectively, and enjoyed in human experience, is when it is delivered and enjoyed by individuals. For these purposes, classes and communities are no more than aggregates of individuals.

Socialists need not feel uncomfortable about accepting these objectives. The hair shirt is generally the garment of the ascetic, not of the practical politician; and even those who choose to wear it do so, not as a universal model for future aspirations, but as a sign of solidarity with those whose condition must be changed for the better. The early leaders of the Labour movement did not, after all, say to their followers and to those whose support they sought, 'Join us and accept a lower standard of living.' Their message was that socialism was a means by which better standards of living in the widest sense, but including higher material standards for individuals and communities, could be delivered to those who had been unfairly disadvantaged in the past.

## FULL EMPLOYMENT

By far the most significant of all the indicators and elements of economic success is full employment. Full employment is of the greatest importance to the community as a whole, since it is the means by which the community maximises its wealth in the widest sense through the proper use of its most important, almost infinitely renewable and expandable resource – the skill of its people. It is the essential characteristic of an economy that is working well.

It is also of the greatest importance to each individual. It is not necessary to take an overly romantic view of the value of work and the dignity of labour (as the saying goes, if work was such a wonderful thing, the rich and powerful would have made sure that they did more of it themselves), but it is nevertheless true that employment – which usually but not necessarily means paid employment – is the means by which the worth of each individual is recognised. It is the means by which the individual can feel self-respect, by virtue of the contribution he or she makes to his or her own support, to that of dependants and to the community as a whole. For most people, though not necessarily for everyone, employment is a means of self-expression and self-fulfilment.

Full employment is also the most important single practical step that can be taken in modern society to diffuse power, to redress the balance between capital and labour and to bring about some form of economic equality. It is, after all, the rise in unemployment which has seen labour at such a disadvantage and which has been the single greatest cause of family poverty and social division. The restoration of full employment would reverse these losses.

Full employment will, of course, mean different things to different societies. In modern Britain, it will not necessarily mean a forty-hour week for forty-eight weeks a year. It will increasingly mean part-time work, flexible hours, employment which varies in hours and form according to the time of life, family circumstances and other interests – including educational requirements – of each individual.

Technological advance is, of course, also likely to mean that the working week and working year will become progressively shorter, as labour becomes comparatively less important in wealth creation. This is in line with long-term trends and the experience of other advanced industrial countries; but we should beware of those who argue that the micro-chip and the robot will make full employment a thing of the past.

There has been no more convenient alibi for Mrs Thatcher than the view that the unemployment which she has created through deliberately applied measures of economic policy is really the consequence of the new technology. The millions of jobs lost through the Thatcher years were destroyed, not by the micro-chip, but by factories closing or working below capacity. It was a loss of competitiveness as a consequence of mistakes in economic policy that was the true cause of unemployment; the goods we wanted to consume were increasingly manufactured elsewhere, providing employment to others rather than to ourselves.

The new technology will, of course, change the nature of employment, making old skills redundant but creating demands for new skills which, in the nature of things, we cannot easily foresee. There will be a move away from heavy manual work and towards greater skill, away from manufacturing (as a source of employment, as distinct from a source of wealth) and towards services. These changes, as I argued earlier, pose problems and create opportunities for labour and for socialism; but they do not of themselves call into question the prime importance of full employment as a policy objective.

Modern conditions will also mean giving a new value to those forms of work that are currently not regarded as employment because they are not paid. This is particularly true of domestic occupations such as bringing up of children and caring for the disabled, which are at present undervalued.

Full employment does not, of course, mean compulsory employment or employment in a set form. What it does mean is economically or socially valuable work for those who want it; and full employment in this sense should be the central objective of a socialist economic policy. There is no particular difficulty in bringing it about. Contrary to the propaganda to which we have been subjected, there are no insuperable technical problems, and other countries, such as Japan and Sweden, have managed to achieve something like full employment with relative ease.

What is really required is the political will to give priority to full employment as an objective of policy. The implied acceptance by the last Labour Government of the apparent inevitability of unemployment, or at least their reluctance to pay the apparent price for full employment, was the single most destructive step taken by that Government. It is time that the Labour Party reaffirmed its commitment to the objective whose fulfilment, more than any other, will diffuse economic power and restore individual self-esteem.

ORGANISING THE ECONOMY

A Labour Government committed to economic success and to improving the economic well-being of all citizens must necessarily take overall responsibility for the management of the economy. This would primarily require a readiness to use the instruments of macro-economic policy – interest rates, exchange rates, fiscal and monetary policy – to ensure that a socialist economic policy succeeded in producing sustainable growth and an efficient use of resources, as a corollary to the achievement of wider socialist aims.

There are those who scorn economic success (and the instruments of macro-economic policy) as being concerned solely with 'the management of capitalism'. We need spend little time in rebutting this view. Critics of this persuasion seem to overlook the fact that economic success is as ardently desired in the so-called socialist countries of Eastern Europe as it is here (ask the citizens of Poland), and that there is no escape from the laws of economics merely by posting a notice to the effect that 'socialism is practised here'.

It may be true that, if we were to opt out altogether from the world economic system, we might escape the need to concern ourselves with matters like interest rates and exchange rates. The price we should pay would, however, be a heavy one in terms of living standards (and, in a democracy, in terms of popular support), and we should not in the end avoid having to juggle with other economic imperatives of an equally pressing kind.

We should straightforwardly acknowledge that the socialist aspiration is to manage the economy successfully and well, and that nothing would do more to increase the appeal of socialist policies than the association of those policies with economic success and rising living standards for all. Nor is there anything incompatible with socialism in such an approach; quite the reverse. It can be argued that the Left is generally more naturally and properly concerned with wealth creation – with the interests, that is, of the true creators of wealth and of those who depend on the creation of wealth for their livelihoods – while the Right is generally more solicitous of the interests of those who own and manipulate wealth, and whose economic well-being does not depend to any large degree on the creation of new wealth.

Indeed, this point is the key to macro-economic policy for any Government of the Left, and particularly for a socialist Government. I have argued already that the restoration of full employment should be the most important step a Labour Government could take to strengthen the position of the wealth creators in relation to the wealth manipulators. I also argue that the technical problems of establishing full employment are easily overcome; but before this task can be tackled with confidence, a socialist Government would have one important issue to resolve.

That issue concerns the relative importance ascribed by Government to the interests of finance as opposed to those of wealth creation. When confronted with this issue, most socialists would have no hesitation in saying that they attach little importance to the financial manipulations of the City of London and are much more concerned with those who create real wealth. Yet the record of Labour governments, and of the Labour Party's own attitudes on this subject, do not bear this out.

The reasons are deeply embedded in our history. By the mid-nineteenth century, Britain was clearly the most powerful industrial and trading economy in the world. As a consequence of that success, we had built up substantial assets around the world and we had developed a pre-eminent financial centre in London where those and other assets could be traded.

We (that is, those whose interests prevailed) grew accustomed to relying upon the very substantial investment income derived from those assets. That income became increasingly important to our national well-being. It meant that we had to pay less attention to actually earning our living; we were therefore less concerned than we might have been as other major economies developed and became more efficient industrial economies than we were. Indeed, the form in which we insisted on being paid the income on our overseas investments – in gold – meant that, because the domestic money supply was linked to the amount of gold, there was a constant inflationary pressure, which progressively made us less and less competitive as a manufacturing economy.

In these circumstances, we naturally attached top priority to the preservation of the assets and of their value, with major consequences for our defence and financial policies. We not only spent much more than comparable economies on the maintenance of armed forces around the world; we also placed more and more value on London's role as a world financial centre.

We were, in other words, an imperial economy, with all that that meant in terms of the relative importance given to wealth preservation and wealth creation. In terms of economic policy, in particular, we fell into the habit of giving absolute priority to the interests of those who held assets and dealt in money, as opposed to those who made and provided goods and services and tried to sell them in international markets. In this respect, we differed markedly from those rival economies that saw their economic future as depending not on wealth preservation, but on wealth creation, and that therefore concentrated on building their strength and competitiveness as manufacturing economies.

It is this that explains our long comparative decline against other economies. While they have concentrated on becoming dynamic and efficient wealth producers, we have been content with maintaining the status quo. That bias in favour of wealth, capital and finance and against industry, production and labour remains today. It has been the leitmotif of British economic policy for over a century. It was Winston Churchill, as Chancellor of the Exchequer, and in the year he returned to the Gold Standard, who said, 'I would rather see Finance less proud and Industry more content.' It is the last vestige of the imperial mentality – surviving even the illusions that kept British forces east of Suez until the 1960s – and it continues to do great damage today.

Much of British social and economic history over the last century can be explained in this light. The characteristic of British economic policy over this period has always been the predilection for policies of financial orthodoxy, the policies that would maintain the value of financial assets and preserve the status of the City of London. British governments have always opted for the Gold Standard, or defending the pound, or monetarism, at whatever cost to the real economy – the economy where new wealth is or ought to be made.

The same attitudes are deeply entrenched in the national psychology and culture. It is almost as though, having initially made our wealth through getting our hands dirty, we have deliberately tried to expunge that experience from the national memory. All the prestige, the high salaries, the best talents, go to the professions, the City, and the Civil Service; manufacturing takes a low priority. The educational system reflects the same values and helps to perpetuate a vicious circle of low achievement, low rewards and low status for wealth creation.

It is so long since we approached economic policy-making on any other basis that it is difficult for policy-makers to understand how peculiar is the British obsession with financial orthodoxy and maintaining the value of assets. We are brought up to see the pound sterling as a virility symbol and an expression of our world role. The very language we use ('the pound had a good day today') encourages us to see economic news from the viewpoint of wealth-holders. Even supposedly radical politicians have difficulty in disentangling themselves from these prejudices, to such a degree that they are not even aware they hold them.

The notion that we might actually use the exchange rate positively in the interests of promoting and maintaining the competitiveness of our industry and extending its productive capacity – something successful economies do as a matter of course – is totally foreign to us. As a consequence, we have no experience of what it might be like to be truly competitive and of what it might mean to plan aggressively to extend market share in the markets that really matter – the international markets for mass-produced goods. When did a British firm last invest in major new capacity, perhaps on a green-field site and developing a new product or technology, with a view to selling substantially to export markets?

We can see the same forces at work in our current economic situation. The response to economic problems – whether they be inflation or the balance of payments – is to raise interest rates, in line with the policies of financial orthodoxy, which suit the interests of the financial establishment. This is done, whatever the consequences may be for industrial investment and, through the impact on the exchange rate, for competitiveness.

It is regarded as axiomatic, for example, that the Bank of

England, in its role as the representative of the banking industry, should have the ear of the Chancellor and should virtually determine policy on these issues. The voice of industry, on the other hand, is muted and uncertain and has very little influence on Government policy. The Confederation of British Industry (CBI) will occasionally bleat about the damage done to manufacturing by high interest rates and the consequent over-valuation of the currency, but little attention is paid to them by the policy-makers.

Labour governments have not been immune to this bias – far from it. It was Ramsay MacDonald who presided over record unemployment and was prepared to cut unemployment benefit in the name of the Gold Standard, virtually destroying the Party in the process. It was Harold Wilson who fatally delayed devaluation in a three-year defence of the parity, which may have pleased the bankers but did great damage to our industrial economy and to Labour's electoral prospects. And it was James Callaghan and Denis Healey who accepted the prime importance of the money supply as the determinant of economic policy, and thereby ushered in a decade of Thatcherism. Who, today, pays any attention to the monthly £M3 figure which, in the late 1970s, dictated economic policy from month to month?

This vulnerability of Labour governments to the interests of the financial establishment is all the odder when one considers the electoral damage it has done the Labour Party and the economic damage it has done Labour supporters. It is, after all, Labour voters in the shops and factories who suffer when the economy is deflated yet again in the name of financial orthodoxy. It is working people who lose their jobs as competitiveness is hit, whose living standards suffer as British industry continues to lose ground and whose services and benefits are cut as the national economy flags. The bankers who benefit from the subservience of Labour governments in this respect invariably do all they can to remove their benefactors from Government.

Labour activists have often been surprisingly unconcerned about this vulnerability. Much attention is constantly paid to the issues of ownership of industrial enterprises, yet the major defeats and failures of Labour governments have come, not because we have failed to nationalise this or that industry, but because Labour chancellors have agreed in response to pressure from the financial institutions to deflate the economy, and thereby to impose on the workers the sole burden of grappling with our deficiencies in international competitiveness.

Past experience seems to have taught us nothing. We hear the same siren voices today, urging that a Labour Government will have to give priority to gaining the confidence of the City by maintaining the value of sterling at all costs. We do not seem to have learnt that the attempt to gain the confidence of the financial establishment is not only futile but is not even desirable. The only condition on which it can even be attempted is the abandonment of our programme, since once we accept the over-riding importance of whatever monetary measure is currently fashionable, the bankers' leash can be tightened at will.

A Labour Government that wished to meet the twin objectives of managing the economy efficiently and putting socialist principles into practice would have to be clear that this bias in favour of financial orthodoxy must be reversed. Giving priority to the wealth-creators is not in itself socialism, but it is a pre-condition of socialism, and it would require a radical departure from past practice and attitudes. It would require a Labour Chancellor to be clear that it was the real economy, rather than the money economy, that mattered, and that it was our task to serve the interests of those who created real wealth.

AN INDUSTRIAL STRATEGY

This realisation should pre-dispose a Labour Government to listen more attentively to industry – both unions and managers – than has been true in the past. The close co-operation between Government and industry – what might be called a medium-term industrial strategy – which has served other economies so well should come naturally to a Labour Government committed to wealth creation. There is clearly great advantage to Government and industry, and to the economy as a whole, if some agreement can be reached on the economic context in which wealth creation can flourish; and this requires a degree of consensus and identification of objectives that is closer to the concept of socialist planning than to right-wing and *laissez-faire* ideas.

British governments have, however, consciously rejected this approach and have thereby adopted, for reasons of ideological prejudice, a course diametrically opposite to that followed by governments in more successful economies. In Japan, for example, Government/industry co-operation has been raised to a very high degree through the agency of the Ministry of International Trade and Industry (MITI). The French and Italians have established a level of mutual confidence between Government and industry totally foreign to anything the British have experienced. Even the Americans, through the immensely important relationship they have established between the defence industry and Government, make sure that Government is heavily involved in their industrial economy.

Only in Britain is a close and co-operative relationship between Government and industry regarded as something to be resisted rather than encouraged. This attitude is the product of ideological blinkers on the part of Government and of prejudice on the part of industry, both fed by an alarming ignorance about the proper role of each in promoting our industrial future.

The problem is exacerbated by the fact that British industry is increasingly unrepresented in the councils of Government. This is partly because industry itself no longer has an effective voice, and partly because Government in this country is accustomed to listening to voices other than that of industry.

British governments have over a long period maintained arrangements whereby, through the Bank of England and the Treasury, the viewpoint of the financial economy impacts directly on ministers. By contrast, the mechanisms by which industry makes its views known to Government have been progressively weakened. The Department of Trade and Industry (DTI) has abdicated from its role as a partner for industry, and the institutions of Government/industry co-operation, such as the National Economic Development Council (NEDC), have been increasingly ignored by ministers. At the same time, the CBI has become increasingly dominated by financial institutions and importers, and even those CBI members who retain

an interest in manufacturing very often carry out their manufacturing abroad.

The peculiar feature of the Thatcher years has not just been
the priority given to the Medium Term Financial Strategy, but
the total absence of an equivalent 'Medium Term Industrial
Strategy'. While great attention has been paid in the past to
irrelevant measures such as £M3, very little attention has been
paid – by the Government at least – to the desirability from
industry's viewpoint of some predictability in matters such as
interest rates and exchange rates, or the projected level of
demand, or even the rate of inflation.

It is surely apparent that industry would benefit from a more
powerful voice on these questions and on issues like trade
policy, or the most appropriate form of incentives to investment. Are our industries adequately protected against dump-
ing? Are investment grants likely to be more effective in
promoting investment than investment allowances? What
would be the most effective form of Government/industry
co-operation in terms of securing the research and development effort we need, or the level of training that will be
necessary?

As long as we fail to address these questions in an effective
forum, one that provides a proper meeting place for Government and industry, we shall continue to handicap ourselves in
the battle to maintain international competitiveness. Our
foreign rivals have shown just how crucial this degree of mutual
confidence can be in promoting industrial success.

A central feature of the most successful industrial policies has
been the concentration on certain sectors. It seems to matter
less which sectors are selected; what matters is that all the
efforts of Government and industry should be concentrated
rather than dispersed. Clearly, such a concentration requires
careful preparation and wide discussion.

That is why the next Labour Government should offer a new
partnership to industry. It should be a partnership based not on
any attempt to dictate to industry, but rather on the great
advantages to be gained through a systematic and institutional-
ised effort to ensure that both sides understand each other and
work with, rather than against, each other. No Government
will promise in advance to do everything that industry wants,

but there is surely much to be said for at least knowing what is in each other's minds and trying to increase the mutual confidence on which longer-term planning – for both Government and industry – can be based.

There will, of course, be those who fear that such a concept of co-operation will merely provide a cloak for corporatism. But if, by rejecting corporatism, we mean that the Government should talk to no one, then that is clearly absurd. What we have at present is not the rejection of corporatism, but corporatism engaged exclusively with the small élite group whose power is based on finance. We cannot afford to be frightened by labels. The danger of corporatism is that democracy is impaired. That is a real danger, and one against which we should be on our guard. But consultation and co-operation do not impair democracy nearly as much as does the long-term damage of a weakened trade union movement, a demoralised workforce and a crippled economy.

A Government prepared to take industry into its confidence and an industry prepared to work with Government can bring great benefits to the national economy. To turn our backs on these advantages would not be a high-minded renunciation of corporatism but would mean resigning ourselves to doing badly what we are trying to do well.

There is one further advantage to be obtained from this new partnership, and one which would in any case militate against the realisation of corporatist fears. An industry that is offered a real role to play in relation to Government will find it necessary and desirable to organise itself rather better than it does at present.

By comparison with other countries, membership by British companies of trade associations, chambers of commerce and so on, is very much a hit and miss affair. A Government that was prepared to work through industry in order to secure an effective industrial strategy would also wish to see, and would therefore positively encourage, the proper and comprehensive organisation of industry at every level. This would involve using bodies such as trade associations and chambers of commerce as partners with Government, and as conduits for the help Government can offer.

This in turn would provide powerful incentives to firms to join such organisations; it would also offer us a decentralising element to counter-act any corporatist tendencies, and an instrument of regional policy. This is very much the case in West Germany, for example, where membership of chambers of commerce is mandatory, and where the chambers fulfil important quasi-governmental functions, such as the organisation of employee training.

An effective industrial strategy will, of course, require more than consultation and co-operation between Government and industry. It will also depend on Government undertaking those responsibilities that cannot be discharged by private firms operating in the free market. This means public investment on basic science and industrial infrastructure; it means organising and co-ordinating industry-wide efforts in training and research and development; it means pump-priming investment, in partnership with industry, in new and leading technologies. A Government which is serious about building our industrial strength must match the efforts and involvement made by the governments of our major competitors.

## THE TRADE UNIONS

One of the most marked characteristics of Tory policy has been the exclusion of trade unions from national counsels and the attack on the legal immunities that have allowed trade unions to match, on behalf of their members, the power of employers. There are many who believe that this assault on the supposed power of the trade unions has been very popular and that the Labour Party cannot hope to recover popular favour unless it disengages itself from the unions.

This is a delusion. The trade unions and the Labour Party are inextricably linked, through history and political outlook, and there is no reason to believe that a divorce at this stage would do anything to help resolve their common problems. This is not to say that their relationship is set in concrete – changes in the means by which the Labour Party is financed and in the Labour Party constitution would almost certainly strengthen rather than harm the relationship – but it does mean that it remains a source of strength, something to be built upon rather than renounced.

For the socialist, there are several wider issues that ought to inform the policies of a Labour Government. There is, first, the question of the role the unions should play in the formulation of national economic policy. It is clearly nonsense, and a ridiculous expression of political prejudice, that the representatives of nine million workers should have been virtually frozen out by the present Government from consultation on economic policy. A Labour Government should bring the unions back into that process of consultation, simply because it makes sense to involve the organised workforce in the decisions that affect their members.

The major issue, however, is the question of whether the trade unions should enjoy any special legal status, and if so on what basis. The detail of trade union law is beyond the scope of this book, but it is possible to give a general and theoretical answer to the question.

A preliminary point should first be made. It was clearly a serious political mistake, and a denial of socialist principle, to allow others to espouse the cause of democratising the trade unions. Democracy and the diffusion of power are central to the socialist project, in the trade unions as elsewhere. Socialists should always be in the van of such developments.

An equally clear answer can be given to the central question. The trade unions need special legal immunities because the ordinary law of contract and tort prevents them from using the only strength they have – the solidarity of their members – to match the otherwise overwhelming power of the employer in the market-place. As long as the wage bargain retains its present form and importance, and capital is placed in a position of advantage in relation to labour, the individual worker is entirely at the mercy of the employer. That imbalance can be made good only by allowing the workers to create and enforce a common interest; and that requires special legal immunity.

The point is seen clearly in the current law regarding secondary action. For many years, trade unions involved in furthering their members' interests in the course of an industrial dispute were entitled to bring pressure to bear on an employer by inflicting or threatening economic damage to a third party with whom the employer had economic relations. This would have been actionable if done by an individual; hence the need for special immunity.

The present law has removed that immunity, and has been speedily exploited by employers, who have found it easy to create different legal identities for different parts of their operations, and thereby to limit workers in many cases to taking industrial action in their own workplace and nowhere else. Given the ease with which modern enterprises can switch production from one plant to another, the power of the trade unions to resist a powerful employer has been virtually neutralised; and the courts have been quick to enforce this new balance of power with injunctions and sequestration orders.

The law appears to have been framed in the belief that most employers conduct small-scale businesses, which need protection from becoming caught up in disputes that do not concern them. The reality is, of course, that the prime beneficiaries of the new law conduct businesses that are complex in structure and are owned by major institutional shareholders with access to the best legal advice and with the ability to juggle their affairs so as to render the trade unions impotent. The consequence has been a major weakening of the already inadequate power of labour and the creation of a labour market which, in the context of mass unemployment, has worked very much to the advantage of already powerful employers.

There is also a great deal of confused thinking on the question of the individual's relationship with the trade union. The Tory Government has long fulminated against the closed shop, and has now announced its intention to outlaw it by legislation. There will be many – including many trade union members – who agree with them.

The starting point for any assessment of the arguments must be the dependence of the trade union on solidarity; every individual who opts out of a trade union and chooses in effect to deal individually with the employer weakens not only his own position, but also that of all his fellow workers. That right is upheld nevertheless by many people, on the grounds that to deny it would be a major blow against the freedom of the individual.

The parallel is drawn with other voluntary organisations. Just as the individual can choose whether or not to join a club or association, so, it is argued, he or she should be free to choose whether or not to join a trade union at the workplace. Some even rely on the fiction that the decision whether or not to work is a voluntary one, and argue that, once at work, the individual's decision on trade union membership should be equally voluntary.

These parallels are not convincing. There is another and more accurate way of looking at the question of the individual's membership of a trade union. That membership is an incident of employment. For most people, employment is not a question of choice but of necessity. The choice is all on the side of the employer. He or she has almost unfettered freedom to decide whether to employ at all, and whether to employ one individual rather than another.

Moreover, having taken employment, the individual is obliged to accept from the employer conditions of employment over which he or she has very little control. It is the employer who ultimately decides how many should work, for what purposes, in what conditions, on what terms, and when the employment should begin and end. All of this is accepted without demur as part of the natural order of things. No question of individual liberty is perceived to arise. The fact that most individuals have little control over eight hours of their waking day is regarded as the product of a free and voluntary bargain struck between equals, and few look behind this myth to the reality.

As soon, however, as it is suggested that, in addition to all the myriad obligations imposed on the employee by the employer and accepted without question, he or she should also accept an obligation imposed by his or her fellow workers – the obligation to belong to a trade union – fundamental questions of individual liberty are said to arise. It is hard to see why. There is no doubt that any obligation is an infringement of liberty, and that the obligation to join a trade union is no exception. Obligations are often accepted, however, because they are seen to meet a valuable social purpose, or because they are seen as fair and reasonable and generally applicable. Why is this not the case with trade union membership?

The answer must be that while we are used to accepting obligations imposed on us by authority figures (including employers), to such an extent that we hardly notice that they infringe our liberty, we are simply not accustomed to accepting obligations from fellow workers. The complaint that the obligation to join a trade union is an unacceptable attack on individual freedom seems to owe more, therefore, to our habits of mind, including our habit of deference to our supposed superiors, than to any fundamental distinction between that obligation and many others.

It is this way of looking at the question of the closed shop and trade union immunities which ought to inform the policies of a Labour Government. We should have no hesitation in recognising and upholding the importance of trade unions in a free society (as Mrs Thatcher does, provided they are not here but in Poland), and in ensuring that the law provides the trade unions with the conditions in which they can operate to protect their members. At the same time, we should take the lead in ensuring that the trade unions operate democratically, and are encouraged to make a responsible contribution to economic policy.

# CHAPTER FIVE

## The Role of the Market

British socialists have long agonised over whether or not to accept that the market might play some role in a modern socialist society. In the *Aims and Values* document produced by the Party in 1988, the frank recognition that the market might be a valuable instrument in the hands of a socialist Government provoked a storm of protest.

Yet it is hard to see why this should be a matter of controversy. There is virtually no society in today's world that does not make some use of markets. The most primitive societies utilise the market, in however rudimentary a form. The centrally planned economies of Eastern Europe are making more room for the market, while China is in the process of transforming itself into a market economy. Even in Albania, the notion that everything can be done by the planner and bureaucrat is today regarded as somewhat eccentric.

The essence of markets is the use of prices to allocate goods and services, and all modern large-scale economies now make some use of this mechanism. Even in the Soviet Union, the system attempted by Lenin between 1918 and 1921, with goods allocated by planning instead of prices, has long since been abandoned. Input allocations and output targets for firms are still largely set by authority, but money payments and prices in the Soviet Union are widely used as instruments for carrying out these decisions, with the allocation of consumer goods and labour being largely (but not exclusively) determined by prices.

The invitation we are sometimes offered, to debate the question of whether socialists in Britain should accept or reject the market concept in its entirety, is therefore a ludicrous piece of self-delusion. By pretending to ourselves that there is a real option – both desirable and practicable – of doing without the market altogether, we engage in a debate that has no meaning anywhere else in the world.

We also do ourselves quite unnecessary damage. We maximise the alarm our opponents can create in the minds of the uncommitted, and we damage our own credibility by seeming to live in a fantasy world totally unrelated to reality. We invite contempt and scorn because we are heard to say what we manifestly do not mean, and because we are seen to make no attempt to act on what we say when we get the chance. We also depress our own morale, since the inevitable concessions we have to make to the market in the real world are seen in the terms we ourselves define as unwelcome defeats forced upon us by our opponents.

We should do much better to acknowledge that the question for us, as for virtually every other society and economy, is not whether or not the market, but where, how, and for what purposes? What tasks can the market perform better than other social and economic mechanisms? Where are markets inappropriate and better replaced – and by what? When and how should they be monitored and regulated? These are the real questions – the questions that matter to socialists and that have to be answered in modern politics.

## THE ADVANTAGES OF THE MARKET

Any consideration of the market as an instrument of socialist policy must begin with the recognition that it is likely to be in many areas a more efficient and acceptable allocator and distributor of scarce resources, and a more sensitive means of meeting consumer preferences, than any system of planning could conceivably be. The market is more powerful and flexible than is possible for any bureaucratic operation, even taking account of the huge advances in computer technology. There is no reason for socialists to deny this obvious truth, which is confirmed by everyone's daily experience.

Markets are, moreover, a way of generating approximations to efficiency prices – those prices that clear markets, that provide more or less accurate information and that inform buyers and sellers of the costs of production in terms of the alternatives that must be forgone. In theory, a perfectly informed planner could set these prices, but no such planner will ever exist and markets are the best rough and ready tool we have. Again, socialists should be quick to recognise the spur to overall efficiency which properly functioning markets provide.

The market also provides a stimulus to innovation, which may go a long way towards explaining the greater dynamism of market-based economies. Markets are, as Le Grand and Estrin say in *Market Socialism*, 'an excellent way of processing information while simultaneously providing incentives to act upon it'. They 'encourage innovation both in production techniques and in the goods themselves' and 'disperse economic power' to a substantial degree, at least as compared with a centrally planned economy.

The decentralisation of economic power which the market encourages should be recognised by socialists as one of the market's most desirable features. It is not, of course, something to be taken for granted, and it can easily – in markets that are not properly monitored and regulated – become more an illusion than a reality. It is nevertheless a feature that is intrinsic to the market, one that socialists should strive to make as effective as possible. We should, in particular, be alert to use the new technology – inter-active electronic communication, for example – to increase the power of each individual to act effectively in the market.

In this sense, therefore, markets are undeniably a potential force for good in the struggle to increase individual freedom. This is not to say that markets automatically operate to this effect – but the potential is there and socialists should recognise it. The task is not to exclude the market but to make sure that, where it is appropriate and useful, it works better and more fairly.

THE MARKET'S PRETENSIONS

There are those on the Right who believe that this is all there is to say, and that these readily acknowledged advantages of the market mean that it is in fact beyond criticism. For them, the market is not only an efficient instrument; it is also a kind of moral arbiter, rewarding the virtuous and punishing the lazy or incompetent, through the application of rules that have an objective and universal validity. On this view, any intervention in the unfettered operation of the market is bound to be unjustified, because it must distort the operation of what is an impartial mechanism, whose judgments cannot be second-guessed.

The great text for such believers is Adam Smith's explanation of the 'invisible hand', though it is doubtful if Smith himself intended his remark to be taken as quite the assertion of the market's infallibility that it is usually taken to be. Nevertheless, it is this view of the market – that the combined effect of a myriad of individual and self-interested decisions produces a result that is in the interests of society as a whole – that gives it its almost mystic authority and commands a semi-religious adherence from its supporters.

It is here, of course, that the socialist and the free-marketeer must immediately part company. The market is not an impartial and objective mechanism handing down judgments that cannot be questioned. It is not independent of society and man-made rules. It is as much a chosen and arranged device as any system of planned allocation. It is simply rather better at covering its tracks.

The market depends on the mechanisms of exchange, the rules of contract law, and in most cases on the rules that define and protect property (though there is no reason why the market should not operate within a system where property is publicly owned). Without socially ordained arrangements, the market could not operate. It is, in other words, just one of a number of instruments that society could choose in order to carry out certain tasks. It has no greater sanctity, or intrinsic moral virtue, or moral independence, or self-sufficiency, than any other system. Like them, it is to be judged purely on results, and if the results are unacceptable or could be better achieved in some other way, the market must give way to other possibilities.

There is no doubt, however, that the view that the market operates independently of human agency is widespread, and that the ability of the market to masquerade in this way adds greatly to its acceptability. Those deprived of a benefit by a bureaucrat will resent it greatly and will naturally conclude that they have been dealt with unfairly and that their liberty has been infringed. The same person who is deprived of the same benefit by an inability to afford it in the market-place will reach no conclusion other than that he or she is unfortunate to lack the necessary purchasing power. Yet, while the market does not determine the precise outcome of every potential allocation, its general operation is just as much organised by the prevailing elements in society as though it were planned in every detail.

The quasi-religious view of the moral authority of the market is, of course, an extreme one, and like many extreme views it features rather more prominently in rhetoric than in the practical programmes pursued by its proponents. It is in fact the mirror image of the total rejection of the market espoused by some on the Left, who would be horrified if they found one day that they could not buy their bread from the corner shop but had to present a coupon instead to the State planning office.

The truth is that governments of all persuasions, including those of the extreme Right, constantly intervene in the market for a variety of purposes. The mere fact that intervention is considered necessary, even if for limited purposes and in limited circumstances, shows that even for governments of the Right the market is far from infallible. It also demonstrates the social and human nature of the market rules, since if intervention is possible in some circumstances, it must also be possible in others, and the decision not to intervene is as much a matter of deliberate policy as the decision to intervene.

THE MARKET'S INEFFICIENCIES

An assessment of the market's strengths and weaknesses can appear to be unbalanced. The strengths are obvious and can largely be taken for granted. The weaknesses are more complex and difficult to disentangle, and take more time to lay bare. The purpose of doing so is not to discredit the market, but to make sure that it is used to the best effect and for the purposes for which it is most appropriate.

The market is first of all deficient simply as a mechanism. It depends for its proper operation on the full availability of information and the taking of rational decisions by market-makers. Neither of these two conditions ever fully applies. As a consequence of imperfect information and irrational responses (sometimes exacerbated by the pressures on individual behaviour exerted by the market itself) we often see the market behave in capricious and extremely volatile ways.

The best examples of this phenomenon are those markets *par excellence* – the markets for shares, foreign exchange and commodities, where the quintessential elements of market operation are seen in their most developed and complex form. It is these market-places that often act in the most irrational and arbitrary way – where market psychology and the herd instinct can produce exaggerated swings (providing, incidentally, a powerful reason for insulating and detaching the broad strategy of macro-economic policy from the short-term vagaries of the money markets).

Markets may also work imperfectly because many individuals may not be able to identify accurately their own self-interest or preferences, or to judge the qualities of the goods and services they buy. This is particularly true in cases such as insurance, financial services, medical care or foods treated with additives. Some consumers – children, the old and the sick – may be unable to take decisions on their own behalf. While it is sometimes possible to buy advice – for example, from the Consumers' Association, or a professional financial advisor – the advice may in practice be inaccessible to or misunderstood by most people, or itself be questionable, or too weak.

The professional ethic of the supplier is often offered as a means of making good these deficiencies, but this is not normally an adequate safeguard. It will need to be reinforced or replaced by State licensing (for example, of doctors and banks) and/or regulation (for example, of financial services or food additives). In general, the greater the cost of consumer mistakes, the greater the need for such reinforcement.

The freedom of consumer choice is also, of course, affected and limited by the discretion exercised by the supplier. This discretion may be influenced against the interests of the consumer because of the incompetence of the supplier in handling market information, or of the market sending conflicting signals to the supplier, or of the supplier's power to dictate, often through advertising, what is available to or desired by the consumer.

Even on the assumption that they work perfectly in their own terms, markets suffer further substantial deficiencies. They are incapable of meeting needs that cannot readily be secured by exchange between individuals in the market-place. They are generally, therefore, bad at securing the provision of public goods – that is, goods that are desired in the interests of the community as a whole but for whose supply no single individual or group of individuals can be found to take responsibility. If goods of this sort are to be provided at all, they thus have to be paid for collectively. This is true of goods such as defence, law and order, or the elimination of infectious disease, and this reasoning can even be extended to more tenuous social goods such as fraternity, equality and stability.

This is partly a question of the essentially individualistic nature of markets and the difficulty they have in representing wider interests. This is not to say that the market cannot be used in such a way as to overcome these difficulties, but a considerable effort of organisation is required in order for the community interest to be able to enter the market-place in an effective way. This will not happen if the market is left to its own devices.

Markets, particularly those in which competition is allowed free rein, impose an inevitable pressure on participants to externalise costs. While it may be possible to use the market device to persuade suppliers to organise so as to share advantages, it is clearly very difficult for the market alone to enjoin the sharing of costs. Again, the market mechanism can be put to use for this purpose – but only after intervention to ensure that the costs or inhibitions are imposed and shared.

A special case of the market's tendency to leave certain sorts of costs uncounted is the perverse reaction to scarcity mentioned by Alec Nove. The price of fish, for example, includes the cost of catching them but not, of course, any cost of the fish themselves. As fish from a particular zone become more scarce, their price rises. This encourages more vigorous fishing, and so the depletion is speeded up.

The market is, paradoxically, as liable to overlook benefits as costs, and this can be just as damaging to the wider interest. For example, a company which devotes resources to a training programme may find that it is benefiting competitors, who poach its staff, and is at the same time losing out in comparative cost terms because of the increased expenditure it undertakes. The net effect is likely to be a refusal by individual firms to train staff, with consequent damage to the economy as a whole.

Just as the market is too fragmented to provide goods to meet wider interests than those of individual participants, so it is also bad at securing longer-term objectives whose provision exceeds the time-scale that individuals would normally accept. The market will respond with alacrity when the individual is offered an exchange that is of value to him or her in the individual time-scale. But when it is a question of long-term investment, and the return on that investment is either generalised, or long-deferred, or uncertain, the exchange value to the individual is not sufficiently precise, immediate or specific to that individual to induce him or her to act.

The market therefore generally fails to provide a good roads system, or adequate industrial infrastructure, or investment in basic science, or investment in longer-term or speculative research, which will benefit the economy as a whole in perhaps hard-to-predict ways. The market's deficiencies are particularly damaging in this respect since it is in these areas that successful economies are active and make essential provision for the future. Again, these weaknesses can be overcome, but only if intervention in the market is organised.

Sometimes what is needed in the wider interest – the redistribution of land to peasants, or war mobilisation, or rapid industrialisation, or the building of a road – will involve a loss for some people as well as gains to the generality. Such goods will not be delivered without intervention, by authority or persuasion, since there is no exchange that can compensate both sides fairly.

These aspects of the market's operations reflect, of course, the fact that the market is an exchange mechanism, which works well only for those who have something to offer and to exchange with others. The market does not respond to those who have nothing to exchange. It is therefore particularly hard on those in modern society who have inadequate purchasing power and who cannot therefore look to the market to provide basic decencies like health care, education and housing. If the market mechanism is still insisted upon, it can work acceptably only if, by virtue of intervention, some attempt is made to ensure that the necessary exchange values are provided to individual participants in the market, through minimum wages, social security payments, subsidies and so on.

This analysis of the market is also helpful in lifting the veil that usually persuades people that the market is value-free and even-handed in its operations. This may well be true – at least substantially – provided the pre-existing disposition of market power is accepted. Once that is given, it may well be argued that the market is an impartial mechanism, which allows to everyone the same opportunity to reach agreement on exchange.

This is, however, an extremely significant proviso. Once its importance is laid bare, it is clear that the market is value-free – at best – only in the sense that it reflects accurately the pre-existing balance of market power. For those who are unhappy with that balance, or who would like to change it in some way, the market is not value-free but is instead a major obstacle to change. Little wonder that the market is the favourite instrument of the Right and of all those who wish to preserve the status quo.

This is also to overlook the natural tendency of the market to increase the power of those who already have power in the market-place. If the parties to an exchange are unequal in their bargaining power, the agreement they reach is likely to reflect the interests, and thereby increase the power, of the party who is already in a position of advantage. An unequal distribution of property rights can make control through exchange at least as coercive as control through authority. The claimed virtue of the market – that it gives to everyone an equal freedom as to whether to enter into an exchange or not – breaks down if the inequality in bargaining power extends not just to variations in the value of what is offered on either side but includes the structure of the market-place and the differing degrees of coercion felt by each participant.

If, for example, the market is one in which one party must secure an agreement, at whatever price, because what is at stake is something essential to civilised life – such as employment, or basic income, or safe housing – then the market can work very unfairly, and is far from being value-free. In those circumstances, the notion of an equal bargain is a fiction; one party has no choice but to enter the agreement, since that is the only way in which the desired benefit can be obtained, and to enter it on terms dictated by the stronger party. Exchange may be 'free' – free from conflict – but it can be free in that sense only because the conflict has already been settled in the existing distribution of property rights. Exchange does not eliminate social conflict in some magic way – the conflict is buried in the existing distribution.

The claim that the market is an instrument and guarantor of individual freedom is therefore fallacious. For many people, the market offers the illusion of free choice but the reality of exploitation and oppression; its only saving grace, which is ruthlessly exploited by its proponents, is that many people believe the illusion rather than recognise the reality.

Markets, like other systems, cost something to run, and although this transaction cost will normally be no more than that involved in planned systems, the volatility of markets can sometimes create excessive uncertainty, which is itself expensive. In some cases, these additional transaction costs are too great to make the market an effective mechanism. At times, for example, volatility in money and foreign exchange markets has created excessive hedging costs for industry, and the volatility of equity markets may have raised the cost of equity finance.

The market response to price changes can also be somewhat capricious. Prices can overshoot, leading to over-investment in successful areas. If changes in demand require new methods, equipment or population distribution, there will be in many cases a time lag before the adjustment is made. This will often create exaggerated prices, and this may in turn lead to exaggerated reactions. Moreover, people respond to other than financial incentives (so that, for example, they do not necessarily roam the world in search of higher paid jobs). This can lead to further lags; the adjustment may happen, but it may take too long, and involve excessive financial and non-financial costs.

Conversely, changes in the market may at the same time call forth a response that is too limited; uncertainty as to future prices may lead to a systematic under-investment and to a bias against risk. Regional imbalance is an instance of this general problem.

Even in their own terms, markets have a natural tendency towards self-destruction – a rather serious design fault, one might have thought, in a mechanism that is sometimes claimed to be infallible. Even Adam Smith recognised the market's natural propensity to produce restraint of trade and monopoly, and that 'People of the same trade seldom meet together, even for merriment and diversion, but the conversation ends in a conspiring against the public, or in some contrivance to raise prices.'

An unfettered or unregulated market will, in other words, exhibit a strong tendency towards eliminating the very virtue – its operation in the public interest – that is often claimed for it. It is for precisely this reason that even the most *laissez-faire* of governments will usually acknowledge the need for an effective competition or anti-trust policy.

Markets also have difficulty in accommodating the desire to avoid some kinds of risk. Thus private markets cannot provide unemployment insurance because of moral hazard – the temptation not to search too vigorously for employment when unemployed. Insurance against congenital disease and previously undetected chronic illness is impossible, since the insurance company knows or will discover on examination that it will have to pay. Private medical insurance is more expensive than it might be because it destroys the budget constraint on doctor and patient.

Companies that are unable to insure against certain risks will often try to replace the market with control – for example, by buying a unique or nearly unique source of essential raw materials or components, or, as a compromise measure, by entering into very long-term contracts. Such options are a function of market power, and as such are not open to most individuals; but they are also means by which the normal functioning of the market is disrupted and made less efficient.

There are also inefficiencies that are peculiar to labour markets. These may create an inflation risk, because it may be impossible for capital and labour to agree on a distribution of added value without increasing that added value, at least in nominal terms – that is, by putting up prices. Markets do not, in other words, always resolve distributional conflict; some form of social intervention may be needed to make things work.

More generally, markets are good at making adjustments to supply and demand at the margin, but they are not so good at organising structural changes, which might involve new methods, equipment, training, attitudes and population distribution. As Estrin and Winter put it in *Market Socialism*, 'while markets may be an excellent tool for fine tuning responses to changing demand and technology, they may not be good at stimulating large, non-marginal changes in the structure of the economy.'

The market may, in other words, be an excellent instrument for offering the consumer a range of choice in the colour of underpants, but it is not necessarily so effective in organising, for example, a strategically appropriate future for the British electronics industry. This is a further instance of the market's inability to take a broad or long-term view.

It is possible that, in a given situation, it would not be in the interests of any one person to change an individual response, but that it would be in everyone's interest for everyone to change to a new pattern of responses. The market, responding as it does only to individual stimuli, could not undertake or produce a change of this nature. It would be left to the Government or some other expression of the collective interest to act as a co-ordinator of information and initiator of the key action that would break the log jam and allow movement towards a new and more technically sophisticated pattern. This may often involve encouraging investment in technologically developing industries, or the creation of companies large enough to compete in world markets. This may be particularly significant when an economy is less developed than rival economies; the effort, cost and risk involved in catching up with more advanced neighbours may be more than mere market stimuli can outweigh.

At a more fundamental level, it may be that the market fails to provide the right kind of psychological stimulation in countries that need to develop rapidly in order to catch up (as

opposed to those pioneering development but at a comparatively slow rate). David Marquand makes a similar point in his
argument for the developmental State. His contention is that
the operation of the market – fragmented, piecemeal,
incremental – was appropriate to the early stages of an
industrial revolution in which we had no competitors; but that
other states which were then faced with the problem of catching
up quickly realised that the market alone could not achieve
what was needed. They recognised the need for a more
systematic and comprehensive approach, in which the State
was necessarily involved as organiser, co-ordinator and pro-
vider of resources.

We, on the other hand, failed to develop any concept of the
developmental State; as other economies overtook us, we
continued and still continue today to hark back to the halcyon
days of free market forces, as though this were the secret of
industrial success. This is in fact the very reverse of the lesson
we should be learning – that the way to gain ground on
competitors who are more advanced is to harness the power of
the State to the enterprise of industry.

This misplaced faith in the market's ability to organise and
co-ordinate unaided a national developmental effort – coupled
with the bias in favour of wealth preservation rather than wealth
creation – has helped to create a national economy that is simply
not up to the task of developing along internationally competitive lines. We cannot expect to become competitive until we see
the market and its true role in a more realistic fashion.

The market has, of course, an important function which
takes us beyond the realm of purely economic relations. As
Lindblom explains, the market or exchange function is a means
of organising society – of providing order and authority – and is
the main alternative with respect to State direction or command.

In this, it has major advantages – of flexibility and the relative
absence of coercion. But there are also costs to be paid. There
is, for example, the point that, in an exchange system, authority
has to give something of value in order to have its wishes carried
out. This may often be a useful check on State power, but it
might also be a means, not available to others, by which the rich

and powerful can exert pressure on and extract concessions from authority.

There is a further point. If some of the functions that might otherwise be undertaken by State authority are entrusted to the exchange mechanism, those who are the major players and most powerful figures in that exchange system will assume some of the character of public officers performing public functions. Society will look to business leaders, for example, not just as successful commercial figures, but as people of authority and responsibility. The mechanism of which they are seen to be custodians also assumes the role of a public institution, and the protection of the State is accordingly afforded to it and to them.

The business community is able to influence Government because it is organised to do so in a way that the individual citizen is not. In Britain, the secrecy surrounding Government makes it more difficult for the citizen to discover enough about what is happening to have any real chance of influencing policy. In addition, the interests of private and State bureaucracies will often converge in certain areas, such as defence, creating the sort of 'bureaucratic symbiosis' that underlies the US military/Government complex.

The State needs the active support of the business community – their initiative and their energy – if it is to achieve its objective of rising national prosperity. The State must thus induce, rather than command. That is indeed the essence of the market system; businessmen must be free to respond as they see fit to economic signals. Lindblom compares the relationship with the mediaeval dualism of Church and State. Conflict is contained – each accepts the other as a dual leader of the system.

The consequence is that the unequal power already enjoyed by the powerful by virtue of their market dominance is reinforced by the power they acquire as quasi-public officers. The State is compelled not just to negotiate with them but to clothe them with some of its own authority. Again, the myth that the market is in every sense a bulwark against State power is revealed. It may serve that purpose for a few powerful individuals, but for others it is merely a means by which State power is suborned to the interests of the already powerful.

## THE NEED TO INTERVENE

For all these reasons, markets cannot be left to operate without supervision. That is why governments of all political persuasions do in fact monitor and regulate markets – with varying degrees of enthusiasm and thoroughness.

Socialists should be ready to tackle the task with a greater degree of scepticism and deliberation than others might bring to it. Socialists should be more than usually alert to the tendency of markets to encourage the concentration of power and to leave the disadvantaged in a position of reinforced powerlessness, and should be less tolerant of the claims made for the market. Where the market's virtues are apparent, the emphasis should be on ensuring that the market delivers those virtues as effectively as possible.

As a consequence, a socialist administration should intervene in the market as a matter of conscious policy and for defined purposes. It should first monitor and regulate the market so as to prevent market abuse and the unfair exploitation of market dominance. This would require, among other things, an effective competition policy and the breaking down of dangerous concentrations of power. We should put in place a powerful anti-trust and anti-monopoly policy, on the US model, particularly in sensitive areas like the Press and the media.

Great attention must be paid to redressing the balance of power between supplier and consumer. This will be partly a matter of stringent rules governing advertising, price fixing and restrictive trade practices generally, and requiring the publication of relevant information; but it also requires a more systematic approach to consumer protection.

The consumer has to be guaranteed better information; better standards have to be established and enforced; more effective inspection and enforcement have to be provided and more effective remedies have to be applied when rules are breached; consumer co-operatives should be encouraged; the consumer voice should be given statutory recognition in the regulation of the major industries serving the consumer; and consumer organisations should be regularly consulted.

It will be objected by those on the Right that this degree of intervention makes it impossible for the market to function.

This view must be firmly rejected; it is one of the strengths of the market as a mechanism that it is able to respond to an infinite variety of inputs, and there is no reason why it should find it difficult to digest measures that deliberately set out to establish a better balance of power.

The need to establish an acceptable balance of power should extend further. The socialist should insist that if the undoubted advantages of the market as an allocative mechanism are to be accepted and utilised, the balance of power of those operating in the market must be constantly reviewed and adjusted.

Major imbalances in purchasing power and in wealth, for example, must be redressed, through redistributive taxation and effective income support. If the market is to be a neutral means of meeting consumer preferences, a deliberate effort must be made to put consumers in a position of greater equality. The operation of the market can, in other words, be used by socialists as a positive spur to achieving the equality they seek.

Nor is it just a question of purchasing power. The rules and circumstances that give some parties to a potential exchange – as in the case of the wage bargain between a powerful employer and an unemployed individual – an unfair advantage must also be changed, so that the exchange mechanism can operate more fairly. This means examining closely the way in which power is distributed (as, for example, between employer and employee), and ensuring – through trade union and employment rights – that the law is used to make that distribution more equal. Only then can the market be trusted to produce acceptable results.

Socialists will also be quick to recognise that there are some areas where the market, although available, is not the most suitable instrument for the purpose in hand. This is obviously true in some areas – markets in children, human organs or dangerous drugs are generally frowned upon, even by the most ardent free-marketeers – but the market's lack of morality and social responsibility also disqualifies it in other cases.

As a means of delivering health care or education, for example, it would certainly be possible to use the market, appropriately adapted, to meet the needs of some people and in some forms; but there are much more obvious, directly available and appropriate non-market solutions, and only an ideologue of the Right would think it worthwhile to put up with the market's imperfections in these fields.

Health care is a case in point. There is a widespread recognition in this country that collective, socially organised provision to meet need – irrespective of purchasing power in the market – is not only the best guarantee of an adequate level of health care to the most vulnerable (who will, as in the case of pensioners, often be the most in need of health care and the least able to pay directly for it), but is also the most efficient and cost-effective means of delivery of health care to the general population. The NHS is supported by the overwhelming majority because it is seen as ethically and practically superior to its market alternatives.

In these circumstances, it seems pointless to strive to introduce the market into health care. The only gain in doing so would be the ideological satisfaction derived from seeing the market prevail, irrespective of its practical and ethical suitability. This is not to say that every vestige of the market must be rigorously excluded on equally ideological grounds. The test should always be the one of practical efficacy; ideology is always stronger if supported by practical advantage. So, there might be a place for market disciplines within the NHS, as a spur to efficiency, provided that the basic and valuable principle of a universally available and free at the point of delivery health service is not damaged or diminished.

Socialists will also be more prepared for, because more ideologically sympathetic to, the proposition that there are some things in modern society that the market alone is virtually incapable of doing. As we saw earlier, the market is not good at providing public goods, like a clean environment or long-term investment, that do not immediately benefit specific individuals; these deficiencies are certain to become more important as society becomes more complex and the simple pattern of exchange between essentially private individuals for immediate private benefit becomes less and less appropriate as a means of meeting society's needs.

These arguments are familiar to socialists and to the general population when it is social provision that is at issue. People are aware of the market's deficiencies in respect of education and health care, and are ready to accept the need for intervention in the interests of the community. It is equally clear when the concern is environmental safety, where the problems demand a collective response, which is much more likely to be made by socialists with their sympathy for collective action. The argument is less familiar when the issue is economic efficiency, yet it is here that it is likely to be at its most compelling.

The market is simply incapable of organising the economy so as to secure strategic objectives in the national interest. The market will not provide the training for skills, or the investment in basic science, or the research and development effort, or the industrial infrastructure, or the application of new technology on a national as opposed to a piecemeal scale, that will be needed by a modern industrial economy which has to meet intensifying international competition.

Free-market ideologues are incapable of intervening effectively or systematically in the market, or of recognising its inability to do certain things. They are therefore ideologically incapable of sponsoring what Marquand calls the developmental State – the State that takes responsibility for ensuring certain things are done, that activity is co-ordinated, that resources are marshalled and organised, that the risk of individual disadvantage from collective effort is neutralised or overridden.

A readiness to intervene in the market in order to secure wide economic objectives is not in itself socialism. It is a characteristic of many regimes that are far from being socialist, since socialism is about more than intervention for the purposes of economic efficiency. It is, however, a major point of difference between ourselves and our right-wing opponents in this country. It is something that is required by and is entirely consistent with our socialist approach to the market, and it has the great advantage of being essential to our future economic well-being.

This is a powerful reason for arguing that socialism, far from being outmoded, as so many commentators and critics argue, is likely to prove more appropriate to modern requirements than a simple reliance on market forces can ever be. There is here an important opportunity for socialists to argue that only by going beyond the deficiencies of the market can we make the long-term and community provision that is essential to our future success, and that only a socialist approach will make good these deficiencies.

Our basic stance should therefore be that there is nothing inherently unsocialist about the market mechanism, if used for well-defined and properly understood purposes, and if properly regulated and monitored. We should be prepared to use it, on account of its great advantages and indeed its superiority over other mechanisms in many fields, but we should also be ready to supplement and by-pass it where necessary – a flexibility that ought to give us considerable advantages over our opponents.

This pragmatic approach to the market will, of course, fail to satisfy those who yearn for the certainties of outright condemnation and ideological extremes. It is, however, likely to serve us rather better in the real world, enabling us to adapt the market to our socialist purposes and to outflank our opponents in the areas where they are most vulnerable and the market least appropriate.

This stance on the market does not prejudice the position we might take on the quite separate question of ownership. The market is, as we have seen, widely used in economies where private ownership is relatively limited. As Lindblom argues, the market could in principle be used as an allocative mechanism, even where all property is publicly owned. Competition and the price mechanism are quite compatible with a publicly owned economy; indeed, there is increasing interest among socialists in the means by which competition among public enterprises can be organised and used to encourage the efficient use of resources.

# CHAPTER SIX

## Diffusing Power Through Ownership

### THE ROLE OF PRIVATE PROPERTY

Socialists have always agonised over the question of private property. For P.-J. Proudhon, famously, 'property is theft'. The private ownership of property and the desire to accumulate property have been the mainspring of capitalism, and therefore of the exploitation of most of those in society who have had no property.

Private ownership and its concomitant – personal aggrandisement – seem to run counter to the socialist concern for the common good rather than individual advancement, and to emphasise the benefits of competition between individuals rather than social co-operation and organisation. Private property is seen to be about material consumption, selfishness and greed. Little wonder that socialists have tended to be ambivalent, if not downright hostile, to the institutions of private property.

This ambivalence and hostility are, however, very much at variance with the aspirations and values of most people in modern society – even those who would in most respects regard themselves as socialists or on the Left. This disparity is one of the most severe handicaps we face in our attempts to secure popular support and to align our socialism with popular aspirations; for if we are fundamentally out of sympathy with the ambitions naturally held by most of our potential supporters, we have little chance of persuading them that we are the right people to represent their interests.

This does seem, however, to be another of those issues where socialists manage to secure for themselves the worst of all worlds – where we tell the world and convince ourselves that we stand for one set of values but, in reality, both in our own personal lives and as a political movement whenever we get the chance, act on a quite different set of values, one which is much more acceptable to the majority.

The time has surely come therefore to regularise our position and to bring our rhetoric more into line with our true principles. To do this, we have to do more than mouth some of the traditional imprecations against private property. We have to decide why it is that we have objections to the theory of private property yet embrace it in practice. We have to analyse the institutions and social functions of private property so as to identify those aspects we find offensive as socialists and those that are compatible with or can be adapted to the socialist purpose.

Much socialist thinking on the subject is at least a century out of date. In pre-industrial Britain, property ownership had a limited significance. For most people, it extended only to the home (in some cases), to rudimentary furniture and personal effects, and to the tools of the trade in the case of a skilled worker. The ownership of this very limited personal property was not seen as an element in the concentration of power, but rather as a defence, which the less powerful could deploy against the pretentions of the more powerful. Property ownership was a means of diffusing power in society and establishing the independence of the small man.

This changed in two ways with the coming of the industrial revolution. The worker found himself, first, giving up his craft, and with it his tools; secondly, the house he lived in with his family was generally owned by the same person as provided him with work in the factory. He became in an almost literal sense property-less, and was, as a consequence, rendered even more powerless in relation to those who did own property.

At the same time, those who did own property, by virtue of pre-existing wealth, accumulated even more of it as the capital process provided its rewards to them. Their property became much greater than could be used or justified by the needs of personal consumption. This surplus privately owned wealth became the capital which financed the capitalist process and which generated yet more wealth in the hands of private individuals. Property became the instrument of division and exploitation – with the chasm between the propertied and the property-less widening all the time.

It was this situation that Marx described and analysed. It was this social and economic role of private property that naturally earned the enmity of socialists. But just as society and economic activity have developed in ways that Marx did not foresee or predict, so the role of private property has developed and become more complex.

Privately owned property remains an important aspect of the mixed economy in which we currently find ourselves. The drive towards the private accumulation of property remains a central mainspring of the capitalist system, but the forms of ownership are now more complex and diffuse.

The most important change, however, is that property owned privately for purposes other than economic investment – in other words, for private consumption – is now much more widespread and is likely to become substantially more so. The rapidly rising incidence of home ownership, now embracing two out of three households in Britain, is one measure of this growth in private property; but almost all households have shared in the growth of privately owned property, whether it takes the form of domestic equipment like cars, television sets and refrigerators, or of assets, which are invested to produce a nest-egg for the future, like building society or other savings accounts.

This growth in the importance of private property reflects, of course, the rising living standards that most people have enjoyed. The trend is, if anything, likely to accelerate. The majority of those who are currently buying their own homes will increasingly be people whose parents have done likewise and who will therefore be in a position to bequeath to them substantial capital sums derived from the sale of the parental home.

These developments call for a reappraisal by socialists of the role of private property in society. Several points should be made. The chasm between the propertied class and those who own no substantial property (particularly those who continue, for reasons of limited financial resources, to rent rather than buy their own homes) is growing wider. The huge increase in the value of residential property has produced an uncovenanted bonus for home-owners. As we have seen, the increase in the market value of their homes is not, however, new wealth; it has, by definition, to come from somewhere. The answer is that it comes by way of transfer from those who do not own their own homes.

Socialists should certainly find this substantial redistribution of wealth in favour of the propertied – subsidised as it is by the taxpayer – both worrying and offensive. It has brought about a redistribution of wealth and power in favour of the well-off that is much more far-reaching and audacious than anything essayed by Labour governments on behalf of the under-privileged.

To object to the precise pattern of redistribution of private property is not the same thing, however, as objecting to the institution itself. The socialist objection to private property has always been to the use of private property as capital – as the means by which the labour of others can be bought and sold and the proceeds of wealth creation appropriated by those who already own property.

For most people today, property does not fulfil that function but is merely a means of personal fulfilment and gratification. We may object to the unequal distribution of these advantages, and to the excessive materialism and ostentatious consumption that accompany them, but property is not in this sense a means of exploitation.

Indeed, it could be argued that, in its modern role, private property has reverted to something much closer to its pre-industrial significance. It is the means by which a formerly property-less proletariat has been re-enfranchised. The industrial worker who lost the ownership of his tools and his home when he moved into the factory and into the house owned by his employer has partly regained a power over his life by virtue of accumulating property.

This role of personal property as a source of individual power and a protection against the claims of others is likely to become increasingly important in modern society. In modern circumstances, the power of other agencies is, unless checked, certain to increase substantially; the multinational company, and above all the State, will extend their power through the use of new technology, because the growing complexity of modern society places a premium on those institutions with the power to impose order.

This prospect arises independently of the political views of those in power. Indeed, as I argued earlier, the threat of an increased concentration of power in the hands of the State or of private institutions is rather greater in the hands of the Right than the Left. The threat arises as a function of modern society.

In these circumstances, the ownership of private property for purely personal purposes becomes an important bulwark against overweening institutional power. It provides at least some element of independence, some localised and personal source of power, which is largely beyond the reach of those who exercise more generalised power. It is, in this sense, entirely consistent with the socialist concern for diffusing power.

What happens, however, when the amount of property owned by many individuals exceeds the amount they need to meet their own personal requirements, however inflated they may be? This may well be the case for many people, as standards of living rise and as the new generation inherits the surplus wealth of the old.

Much of that surplus wealth will find its way, either directly through individual shareholding or business ownership or indirectly through forms of saving, which are then used for institutional investment, into the ownership of our industrial economy. Does this mean that private property is again about to change its role and to become again – even in the hands of millions of individuals – a means of concentrating power, which socialists should worry about?

The answer is surely that this development is something that socialists should welcome and mould to our own purposes. As I argue in Chapter Seven, below, we should recognise the wider ownership of industry as an important step towards the diffusion of power. The new providers of capital are very different from the old-style capitalists. They do not seek the exclusivity of power that the old capitalists enjoyed.

It is inevitable and right that in modern society capital should come from the personal savings of millions of ordinary people. Socialists should concentrate on ensuring that the rights that normally accompany the provision of capital are not somehow detached from the new owners and do not end up under the control of the traditional capitalists.

This is not to say that there are no dangers in these developments. Just as the unequal distribution of wealth creates problems for social cohesion, in the sense that some are able to afford a much higher level of personal consumption than others, so there are even more serious problems if that unequal distribution means that many people – perhaps a majority – become in some senses the new owners of industry, leaving a sizeable minority disfranchised, property-less and powerless.

The modern problem may be, in other words, not so much how to reduce the immense differential power of a tiny minority of exploitative capitalists, as how to ensure that a substantial underclass is not left behind as society itself becomes more affluent and the majority obtain more power. The proper response of the socialist is not to try to inhibit the growing power of the majority. Such an attempt would be futile and would condemn socialism to the forfeit of popular support, but it would also and in any case be a contradiction of the socialist objective of diffusing power.

The proper socialist response is to carry the process further, to extend the new power and the new enfranchisement to everyone, and not just to a section of society – however large that section may be. Here is a project which is not only consistent with the socialist purpose, but which can be achieved only through socialist policy – through a determination to ensure that social and economic power is widely diffused and as nearly as possible equally shared. Here is the means by which socialists can align themselves enthusiastically with the aspirations of the newly successful and propertied, while at the same time remaining true to our traditional socialist concern for the rights and powers of the under-privileged.

DOES OWNERSHIP MATTER?

If the socialist project is, as I argue, essentially about the diffusion and equitable distribution of social and economic power, then one of the most important challenges to socialists remains the ownership of that form of property – capital – which can be used to create new property and which consequently brings with it control over wealth creation in general. This is the form of property whose ownership has been most jealously guarded and limited so that, by virtue of its inherent tendency towards concentration, it has been historically the major factor in the unequal distribution of power.

The exclusive nature of this ownership has, of course, been modified over recent times. It nevertheless remains the single most important expression of the concentration of power in modern society. The current pattern of industrial ownership is the major challenge to any socialist aim of diffusing power. How is this to be tackled – head on, by means of transferring ownership into other and more numerous or representative hands, or, more obliquely, by leaving ownership untouched but by identifying and dealing separately with some of the incidents of ownership, and by increasing the power of non-owners such as employees and consumers?

Ownership is a legal concept which is difficult of definition. On one view, it is simply a term or concept applied to a bundle of rights. According to this view, ownership is merely a shorthand for describing various powers of control over property. Those powers can be, and indeed are, substantially modified – by the rights of others and by the intervention of the State and other agencies. They depend on the rules established by society, and those rules can always be changed either in whole or in part, either generally or specifically.

This offers the prospect of securing the desired outcome in given cases without necessarily having to confront the whole concept of ownership. Tackling ownership itself can often mean difficult practical and electoral questions – confiscation or compensation, for example, and if compensation, how much, and how financed. How much easier to change the rules where appropriate, to limit or modify particular rights or powers, so that the incidents of ownership are acted upon, rather than the ownership itself.

And if ownership is really just a bundle of rights and powers each of which can be modified in various ways, is there not a further way of modifying it, through increasing the rights and powers of others? Can we not, in other words, transfer to or create in others, not ownership itself but some of the incidents of ownership? Can we not redress the imbalance in power between owners on the one hand and consumers and employees on the other by leaving ownership as it is but by increasing the rights and powers of non-owners?

There is a great deal to these arguments, and socialists should be very aware of their possibilities. I shall explore some of them in Chapter Eight, below. At the very least, they demonstrate that there is no particular magic about ownership. They show that we must not be unduly impressed or misled by labels (particularly those invented by our opponents) but should always look to the reality and to the practical questions of how best to secure our objectives. If socialism can be achieved, at least in part, by bypassing ownership, what is wrong with that?

The fact remains, however, that ownership itself will often be central to the socialist argument, as a comprehensive statement of the very rights and powers that are concentrated in a few hands when they ought to be more widely dispersed. There will be many cases where, for the purposes of both analysis and action, it is ownership itself that is at issue; and where only a transfer of ownership will meet the socialist purpose.

THE EXPERIENCE OF PUBLIC OWNERSHIP

The terms 'public ownership', 'common ownership' and 'social ownership' are more or less interchangeable. Each has, however, a slightly different nuance. 'Public ownership' is usually used in contra-distinction to private ownership, but also has a more specific sense of signifying full-scale State or national ownership. 'Social ownership' is a term that has been adopted more recently, as a means both of avoiding what are thought to be the unfavourable connotations of public ownership and nationalisation, and of signifying the range of different forms – other than nationalisation – public ownership can take.

My own preference is for 'common ownership'. This has the considerable merit of being the term used in Clause Four of the Labour Party's constitution:

> To secure for the workers by hand or by brain the full fruits of their industry and the most equitable distribution thereof that may be possible upon the basis of the common ownership of the means of production, distribution and exchange, and the best obtainable system of popular administration and control of each industry of service.

Clause Four remains the best and most widely accepted definition of Labour's aims; it is regrettable that so many who pray it in aid seem so unfamiliar with its provisions. In its use of the term 'common ownership', Clause Four signifies not only the breadth but also the flexibility of the concept. We have everything to gain from maintaining those elements.

On these issues, as on others, an excessive attachment to dogma has led us into a Thatcherite trap. As a consequence of our vulnerability to the insistence by some activists that Clause Four refers exclusively to nationalisation, we have allowed our opponents to develop the argument about ownership in a way that is most favourable to them.

In the Thatcherite view, there is a rigid distinction between private ownership in all its forms on the one hand, and public ownership, which can take only one form – nationalisation – on the other. The only argument is as to where the dividing line should be drawn; and on that question, Mrs Thatcher has been rather more successful than we have in pushing the line back in the direction she wishes it to go.

This is partly a consequence of the general hegemony she has established, but more particularly because nationalisation has not been as successful as we might have hoped. Nationalised industries have not transformed the economy as we expected; they have not delivered the greater sense of participation and popular control which we aimed at. They have not proved popular with the general public.

This is partly unfair. Nationalised industries have on many counts out-performed private industry. Their record on productivity, exports and investment has been comparatively very good. They have maintained national capacity in strategic industries that might have been lost under private ownership, and have also been more responsive to the national interest.

They have been victims, too, of a long campaign of denigration, in which people have been encouraged to add up their perceived failures into a damaging total. Whereas the myriad and continuing failures of private enterprise – both in terms of national performance and of service to individual consumers – are somehow regarded as specific to the enterprise concerned, the failures of public enterprises are constantly recorded and attributed back to the fact of public ownership.

Making all due allowance for these factors, however, the fact remains that the Morrisonian State corporation – the nationalised industry – has been a disappointment. It has in general manifested all the predictable weaknesses of any large organisation, compounded by variable and unpredictable political interference, and providing few of the expected gains in popular control or service to the consumer. As we approach the question of common ownership in the 1990s, it would be pointless and self-defeating to ignore the lessons of this experience.

It is also tactically mistaken of us to insist that we are intent on doing no more than reverting to the status quo ante, and on reversing all that Mrs Thatcher has done. We may well wish to undo in various ways the privatisation programme which the present Government has carried through; but if we insist on treating that programme as though it were a video recording, which we shall simply play in reverse when we return to power, we cannot be surprised if we are seen as backward-looking, bereft of new ideas and unwilling to learn from experience.

We have the opportunity to exploit the inevitable loss of enthusiasm for privatisation that is already apparent and that will gather pace as the privatisers are compelled to move into less and less hospitable territory. The consumers' disenchantment with the priority given by British Telecom to profit rather than the domestic customer, the fiasco of the BP flotation, and the widespread political opposition to and public unease about the privatisation of gas, water and electricity all suggest that the high-water mark of privatisation has already been reached. The Government is now operating on the far fringes of its own dogma. Privatisation is no longer perceived as mainstream politics.

Now is the time to begin the counter-attack and to make the case for common ownership in all its forms. We can build on the growing public perception that private ownership is not the right answer in all cases, but we must also learn the lessons from our experience of public ownership. We must look for forms of common ownership that are more flexible and sensitive to consumer needs, more efficient in their use of resources, more accountable to their employees, better prepared to face competition from other enterprises. Above all, we must understand that ownership is not an end but a means, and that forms of ownership must be judged on the extent to which they diffuse power and promote social justice and efficiency.

## THE MAJOR UTILITIES

The great utilities – water, gas, electricity, roads, rail, telecommunications, postal services – are best suited to public ownership for a number of reasons. They are, as is often stated, natural monopolies. While it is conceivable that rival enterprises might be able to offer competitive services in some parts of their operations, it is hard to believe that there could be – in a rational world – more than one supplier of these services to the nation as a whole.

It is important to distinguish between this point and a number of related points. The assertion that the great utilities are natural monopolies is not invalidated by accepting, for instance, that the best way of organising these enterprises is on a decentralised basis – splitting up their management so that they operate not as huge centralised corporations but as quasi-autonomous regional or local bodies. Nor need it mean that the relations between constituent parts of the enterprise should not be organised on a market or competitive basis, if that were thought appropriate. Indeed, the notion of competition between public enterprises is one that should be further explored.

It is also true that some forms of competition between commercially separate entities could, with difficulty and at a considerable price, be applied even in these cases of natural monopoly. A system of franchises, in which the competition was between those tendering for the franchise, could be imagined. The removal of statutorily protected monopolies, as in the case of postal services, could also mean competition on a purely commercial basis in those areas of service (normally the most profitable) that were attractive to other enterprises, but this could happen in most cases only at considerable cost to the integrity, social function and cross-subsidisation capacity of the basic monopoly.

It would, of course, be possible to subject privately owned

monopolies to regulation and controls, so that they were made
to supplant the usual objectives of private ownership in order to
meet public purposes. But why bother? If the natural and most
obviously appropriate form of ownership for an enterprise that
is public in every other aspect is a form of public ownership,
why go through all the convoluted, unnatural and only partly
successful distortions of the true nature of private ownership?
Dogs can no doubt be taught to walk on their two hind legs, but
no one supposes they can perform as efficiently on two legs as
on four – and if it is then necessary to provide them with
crutches as well, why not accept that they are naturally
four-footed creatures?

So it is with the major utilities. They are inherently
unsuitable to be governed by the exigencies of the market; they
should not be required to behave like privately owned companies, withholding services from those who cannot afford to
pay, charging always what the market will bear, maximising
profit, investing only where there is an immediate return.

The fact is that the great utilities are indeed best served by
single enterprises. The dangers of transferring those monopoly
or quasi-monopoly positions to private ownership are well
understood and, many would say, well illustrated by the
consumer experience of a privatised BT. Some means has to be
found, and public ownership is an obvious candidate, of
ensuring that the consumer is protected against the abuse of
monopoly power. It is one of the major criticisms of privatisation that it has so often meant private monopoly, with all the
attendant dangers, rather than the much-touted liberalisation
and increased competition of Tory propaganda.

It is not just the protection of the consumer against private
monopoly that is at issue. Public ownership of national utilities
is also perceived as appropriate because of the nature of the
services they provide. These services are typically in universal
demand; they provide the essentials of civilised life. They are
services that people cannot choose to go without. They are
services for society as a whole, and they are seen as produced by
society as a whole. It somehow offends common sense and any
sense of propriety that these basic services should be regarded
as commercial goods to be selected or rejected by the consumer
in a competitive market.

Closely related to this point is the fact that the utilities necessarily fulfil a social as well as a commercial function. On ordinary commercial principles, many people would find their basic services being offered to them, if at all, at prohibitive prices, because the cost of provision, and therefore the market price, would exceed their ability to pay. The ability of the major utilities to cross-subsidise, and their obligation to provide a uniform level of service, are clearly of the greatest social importance.

There are various ways of handling this issue. It is often said that financial management is made more problematic by the difficulty of setting financial targets when social functions are deemed to have priority. This problem can, of course, be overcome by separating out and putting a commercial value to the 'public service obligation' – by separating out, quantifying and providing a subsidy for the public service obligation, as has been done with some success in the case of British Rail. It is then possible to establish stringent financial targets on ordinary management principles, quite independently of the public service obligation.

The social dimension is, of course, not the only one that matters. The major utilities have a purely economic importance to the nation, which means that they cannot be regarded as on all fours with ordinary enterprises. Just as the need to meet minimum standards of service to each consumer makes the normal dictates of commercial competition, cost-cutting and profit-enhancement inappropriate, so does the dependence of the economy as a whole on the reliable provision of gas, water, electricity, postal, road and rail communications and telecommunications mean that the national interest must be strongly represented in the decision-making of each enterprise.

These enterprises simply cannot be allowed either to fail, in whole or in part, or to cut the level of their service in response to purely market pressures. This argument in the case of the major utilities can, of course, be extended to other enterprises that are of strategic importance to the national economy – such as the defence industries – or industries such as steel that have 'failed the nation' under private ownership, or industries that supply important non-renewable resources such as coal.

The major utilities are, moreover, very often created in some sense by public enterprise and financed by public investment. The great networks on which gas, water and electricity, or rail, postal services and telecommunications are based are essentially, in modern times, an infrastructure created by the public purse; it is no accident that, even where they originated in private investment and private ownership, they passed into public ownership in many cases because they were seen as 'failing the nation', in the sense that private investment was inadequate to maintain the required level of service to the consumer or to the national economy. The owners for the time being must be regarded as trustees of those resources. They should not feel free to exhaust them, or to milk them for private profit.

Furthermore, the investment which will be required in the future if these resources are to be maintained and developed, and if new resources are to be added, is unlikely to be made by private owners. The history of private ownership in Britain in particular has too often been one of eating the seed corn and failing to provide for the future. The scale of investment required in a modern society to move forward with new projects, like the broad-band cabling of Britain so that each citizen can take full advantage of the new inter-active possibilities of telecommunications, is so great that it is unrealistic to look to private owners to undertake it.

In cases like this – or, for that matter, in the construction of a high-speed rail link to the Channel tunnel that adequately protects the environment – the investment required is essentially in the public interest. The benefits are to the community as a whole. Private ownership and market forces may in some senses be appropriate to the efficient management of existing resources, but the private sector cannot be expected to make the necessary investment in what are essentially public goods.

HOW SHOULD PUBLIC OWNERSHIP BE ACHIEVED?

All other things being equal, then, the case for some form of public ownership of the major utilities is a powerful one. It is for this reason that we have resisted Thatcherite privatisation. These arguments, and the experience of privatisation, show that we are right to insist that gas, water, electricity, postal services and telecommunications should be treated as public assets and services to the community as a whole, and recent polls show that this is increasingly the view of the public as a whole.

The fact is, though, that however we may wish it otherwise, many of the major utilities are now in private ownership, and we shall have to make, when we return to Government, an immediate and practical policy response to that situation. We shall have to answer questions as to whether a return to public ownership is the only or most practicable solution, and as to how, if some form of public ownership is to be sought, it is to be achieved, and what form it should take.

Financial considerations and practical questions of legislative time may lead us to look at solutions other than ownership, at least in the short term; but even where we decide that ownership is the objective, it need not mean in every case a 100 per cent ownership of the full equity in an enterprise. A majority or even substantial minority shareholding will often provide the full control that full ownership would bring; indeed, a 30 per cent shareholding is recognised in the City's Takeover Code as the point at which full control passes.

This option is of particular interest, of course, in those cases where the public retain an equity stake in privatised enterprises, as is the case with British Telecom and may also be true of water and electricity. A majority or controlling shareholding would be a relatively inexpensive means of re-establishing public ownership and control.

In the past, the Labour Party has been concerned that to take only a partial, even if controlling, shareholding would be inadequate, since the law would require the controlling shareholders to act in the interests of the shareholders as a whole. This would mean that the commercial interests of the minority shareholders could not be ignored. A Labour Government that wished to use a partial shareholding in order to pursue the public interest might therefore find itself frustrated by legal action on the part of the minority shareholders, who might argue successfully that their commercial interests were being sacrificed to non-commercial purposes.

It seems unlikely that this need be a real obstacle. It would in most conceivable circumstances be relatively easy to show that the interests of minority shareholders were not so much at variance with those of the majority that the intervention of the courts was necessary to protect them. This would be particularly true where the minority shareholdings were purchased in the open market and in the full knowledge of the priorities of the controlling shareholders and the full purposes of the enterprise.

To the extent that there was nevertheless a real inhibition to the use of partial shareholdings, it might be possible to calculate and compensate for the loss suffered by existing minority shareholders. If necessary, changes in company law could be made to allow enterprises, perhaps in particular categories, to take account of wider, public-interest, considerations.

Whatever proportion of the equity might be acquired, the question of the terms on which it would be acquired would arise. The Labour Party has in the past flirted with ideas of confiscation or, at the very least, with the notion of compensation based 'on need' or excluding 'speculative profit'. This has partly reflected the distaste of Party activists for the notion of private shareholding, and partly been intended to deter people from participating in privatisation issues. It has to be said that these ideas have been unfortunate from the electoral viewpoint and have been totally ineffectual in securing their declared practical aims.

It was the attempt to limit compensation by excluding 'speculative gain' that led the Labour Party into the convolutions of its 1986 proposals for taking British Telecom back into public ownership. The Party felt compelled by a Conference resolution to make it appear that those who wished to exchange their shares for cash would receive no more than the 130p they had paid for them.

The problem was that the real speculators – those who had bought the shares in order to sell them on for a virtually overnight capital gain – had long since done so and departed the scene. They were well beyond the reach of any compensation arrangements offered by the Labour Party.

The only people notionally affected by the Labour Party's strictures were those who were manifestly not speculators – those who had stuck with their investment, very often because they were employees of the company. They were not likely to take kindly to being arraigned and threatened with penalties of an apparently confiscatory nature. The threat was also, of course, more apparent than real, since the offer of 130p per share by way of compensation was not one that anyone in his or her right mind was likely to take up. All that the shareholder had to do to secure more satisfactory arrangements was to indicate a willingness to hold the shares for a little longer.

The whole episode is, however, a prime example of how the Labour Party can get things wrong. For motives that were at best confused and at worst malevolent and doctrinaire, the Party was forced into making empty threats to the wrong (because in every sense innocent) group of people whose political support we should normally have expected. Having postured to maximum effect and maximum damage to the Party's interests, we then proposed in real terms a complicated but reasonably fair compensation arrangement, which, because of our earlier posturing, was easily misrepresented by our opponents and used by them to arouse anti-Labour sentiment, not only amongst BT shareholders but more generally as well.

The proposition that the Labour Party should either confiscate people's property or should compensate at less than a fair market value is in any case so misguided as to be laughable. It is in the first place totally at variance with our general political stance – our commitment to justice and the rule of law. Secondly, as we have seen from the BT episode, it appeared to strike at perfectly innocent people – those who either as direct investors (and often as employees) or through their pension funds had made a perfectly legitimate investment of part of their life's savings.

In electoral terms, the stance was naturally disastrous. It was one of the aspects of our policy that made us unelectable. In any case, it was totally impractical. Any aggrieved shareholder to whom these arrangements had been applied would have had an unassailable case before the European Court of Human Rights (if not the British courts). The only escape from this would have been to withdraw from the European Convention on Human Rights, or at the very least to terminate the right of individual petition – hardly an edifying spectacle for a Labour Government supposedly concerned for social justice and individual rights.

The conclusion must be that where the chosen route to public ownership and control is to acquire the property of others, that acquisition must be on the basis of fair compensation. This means the application of real resources – that is, resources that could have another application – to the purpose.

In principle, this need be no deterrent. The public owners would carry out a transaction in exactly the same way as would any other purchaser. One balance sheet asset – money – would be exchanged for another of more or less equal value – equity. The money for the purchase would be raised in the normal way, either from the purchaser's own resources or by borrowing, often against the security of the asset to be acquired, just as investors in the private sector do.

As a balance sheet transaction, therefore, the purchase of privately owned equity for the public account is not open to objection. It is undeniable, however, that money applied to that purpose could not be applied to another; even borrowing capacity has its limits. The total cost of buying back the equity that has been privatised would amount to something like £40 billion. While the end result would be assets worth roughly £40 billion in the public account, we have to ask ourselves whether this should be the first call on the resources available to a Labour Government? Is a mere change in ownership worth the pre-empting of resources of this magnitude?

There must be a premium on solutions that bring the degree of ownership or control we need but that are less expensive. This means, as we have seen, majority shareholdings, or even minority shareholdings. It means using existing shareholdings, supplemented by new purchases where necessary, more effectively. It means utilising devices like golden shares. It means separating the question of ownership of shares from the totality of the incidents of ownership and control.

We need feel little inhibition in these matters. It is, after all, a Tory Government that has made great use of devices like the special or golden share and has thereby extended the notion that ownership of the equity and the powers of control are not necessarily the same thing. The special share, it is worth recalling, is one that may have a minimal value in equity terms but that carries with it special voting (and usually majority) rights, which can be deployed for the decision of certain issues.

Where a Labour Government either inherits or is able to construct shareholdings of this type, we should be ready to make a reality of the control which in Tory hands – as in cases like Britoil – has been little more than a mirage. A special share arrangement can, after all, be tailored to meet almost any requirement (at present it is usually limited to the admittedly important questions of control – the ability to resist takeover and the restriction of the size of individual shareholdings); there is no reason why it should not have a wider and more effective application in our hands.

Special share arrangements have a further advantage. They have been put in place by Tory governments in cases where the Tories themselves have insisted that the enterprises concerned are properly part of the private sector. Their acceptability in the articles of association of major private companies has therefore been sanctified by Tory practice. If they do a useful job in these few instances – British Aerospace, Rolls-Royce, British Steel, BT, among others – why should they not be extended to other parts of the private sector?

There is, however, a practical obstacle to the extension of special shares. They have, so far at any rate, been put in place by means of altering the articles of association at the behest of a majority or sole shareholder, rather than by legislation. This means that they are available on the present model only in cases where the public already has control. Their prime value seems likely therefore to be in enterprises where they have been put in place before, or in preparation for, privatisation.

The use of such devices, together with partial shareholdings where appropriate, should in many cases provide us with the necessary degree of ownership and control. There will be others, however, where we may feel that we want a greater degree of ownership, without, of course, paying the cost of buying the full equity. In those instances, we might revive the basic proposals of the 1986 document on social ownership, and divide shareholdings into two categories – those in public hands, which would enjoy a monopoly or at least a majority of voting rights, and others, which would continue to produce income, to have a capital value and to be marketable in the ordinary way.

Private shareholdings in this scheme would retain their value as investments. They would cease, however, to be a means by which the full rights of ownership and control could be exercised over the enterprise; in that sense they would take up much more the character of other forms of investment, which have a money value as investments but carry no correlative rights over wider matters.

There could be no problem in the case of new purchasers, who would know very well the nature of the investment they were making, and little cause for complaint on the part of existing shareholders, whose rights are in any case already limited in some instances by the existence of a golden share, and who, judging by their attendance at shareholders meetings, attach little importance to their wider rights as shareholders. It is indeed a familiar complaint against institutional shareholders that they deliberately detach themselves from their theoretical responsibilities as shareholders and prefer to regard themselves as impersonal investors, moving from one investment to another according to strictly investment criteria.

It is arguable, of course, and the argument would certainly be made, that the voting rights attached to shares do have a quantifiable money value, and that the removal of those rights would reduce the value of existing shareholdings by an appreciable amount. That argument ought to be considered; if persuasive actuarial evidence can be provided, there might be a case for making a small once-for-all payment to existing shareholders to compensate them for the loss of voting rights and the consequent fall in value of their shares. Care would have to be taken, however, to restrict compensation to this criterion; changes in the value of shares by virtue of other factors, including changes of control over the enterprise, are, of course, part of the normal hazards of shareholding. The total compensation costs calculated on this basis would remain small and need not deter those responsible for the public purse.

From the viewpoint of the socialist, there is an additional benefit from this approach. The separation of capital ownership and the power of control provides a model of what ought to have wider application. Under this arrangement, capital would become just one more element of production, with no special privileges. The capitalist would expect to receive the market price for his or her capital; to the extent that capital appreciation as well as income was received, this would be a more than adequate recognition of capital's importance. The notion that the provision of capital does not bring with it all the rights of ownership and control is one we should extend throughout the economy.

The key to the issue is flexibility and pragmatism. The objective is what matters, not the means by which it is achieved. What we seek from public ownership is not a particular form; there is no special magic about 100 per cent public ownership, nor anything particularly reprehensible, as we have seen, about private property and investment. The point of public or common ownership is to secure certain social benefits – greater accountability and responsibility, less capriciousness and narrowness. We should concentrate on those aims, rather than dealing arbitrarily with people's property for no good reason. As we shall see in Chapter Eight, below, when we come to consider acting in the interests of the consumer, there may be other steps to be taken in the field of regulation that would, for most purposes, be equally effective and that would not confront us with some of the practical problems of bringing about changes in ownership.

# CHAPTER SEVEN

## *Democratising the Enterprise*

### COMMON OWNERSHIP FOR THE WHOLE ECONOMY

If we are confident, as we should be, of the advantages of common ownership, we should not too easily accept the Thatcherite view that common ownership can only ever be considered (if only to be rejected) in what is traditionally the public sector. There is another range of arguments – for different forms of common ownership – which should encourage us to extend common ownership right across the economy.

These arguments are not so much for common ownership on grounds of community control, as for some form of collective ownership on the part of those whose livelihoods depend on the enterprise. They are not arguments limited, in other words, to those enterprises that can be regarded as in some sense community property, but can be extended to any form of enterprise in which more than a small number are engaged.

These arguments rest very firmly on the socialist concern to diffuse power. They bear upon the relationship of the individual with the enterprise that provides him or her with employment and a livelihood. They concern the nature of labour and its contribution to wealth creation.

The socialist should always be ready to contest the unique privileges that attach to the provision of capital and the relatively powerless position of those who contribute their labour. The power to determine the future of the enterprise, the way it behaves, the products it makes, the people it employs, what to do with its profits – all this is denied to most people who work in an enterprise. That power is reserved exclusively for those who own the enterprise – people or institutions who might in any ordinary sense have very little to do with it but who contribute, perhaps on a merely short-term and partial basis, the capital needed to finance its operations.

To remove this exclusive power from the hands of the capitalist and to vest it instead in those – employees, consumers, ratepayers – who have a more direct interest in the enterprise is a means of diffusing power and of making it more real in the lives of ordinary people. It can be done either by transferring power from capital to labour or others, or by vesting capital in the hands of those who would not normally own it.

There are, of course, socialists who deliberately show little interest in these further possibilities of common or public ownership. For them, public ownership can mean only the full-scale nationalisation of massive, centralised enterprises; to the extent that there might be some part of the economy that did not fall within this category, it would be of no consequence and could be ignored in socialist theory.

The reality is very different. The modern economy is likely to become less and less a matter of huge, centralised enterprises, in which there is a rigid distinction between the interests of the providers of capital and those who contribute their labour. In many instances, the most dynamic and fast-growing sectors of the economy will be those where new technology will be developed and applied in relatively small units, and where capital and labour will work closely together with a greater unity of outlook and purpose than is commonly found in more traditional enterprises. It is here that the concept of a post-Fordist economy has considerable validity and significance.

To ignore this sector, by implicitly accepting that socialists have nothing to say about it, is to pass up a great opportunity. It is in this area of the economy that socialism, and its advocacy of common ownership, has its more fertile and rewarding ground.

Common ownership in this area is to be argued for, not so much on the grounds that are appropriate to large enterprises such as the national utilities, as for reasons of autonomy, choice, freedom, power and control – the issues at the heart of the socialist concern. It is here that the weaknesses of the capitalist insistence on the special privileges of capital, with the consequent denial to the individual of real control over his or her working life, are seen at their most specific and pointed.

It is not as though there is any shortage of ideas. The Labour movement has already developed a fund of experience of different forms of socialism, and socialist movements in other countries – often with more successful records in Government than we can show – can provide us with models we should be foolish to ignore.

Not all of these ideas will be universally applicable or suited to all purposes. Socialism is not, however, about adopting some unique blueprint, appropriate to all conditions and all societies. There is no single socialist institution that will transform the whole of society, providing the one legitimate template for the corner shop and the mass production factory, the Third World smallholding and the high-tech science park.

We must recognise that the socialist response can be almost infinitely flexible and varied, and that this should be welcomed as a strength, not tolerated as a necessary weakness. We should revel in the glorious profusion of socialist ideas, and be ready to entertain new ones – allowing our socialist principles and values to throw up new solutions to developing practical problems and issues.

We can learn from what the Labour movement has achieved in the realms of worker and consumer co-operatives, municipal enterprises (including, very importantly, the enterprise boards), and employee share ownership schemes. Much of what has been achieved in these fields has been a response to unpropitious circumstances. Labour local authorities, in particular, have developed a new range of activities designed to stimulate and encourage their local economies, notwithstanding the attack on their powers, resources and standing from Thatcherite central Government, and in some ways as a necessary reaction to the constraints and bleak outlook imposed by macro-economic policy.

We can explore the possibilities of regional development corporations and agencies, of interventionist and holding institutions like the National Enterprise Board, and of pension funds as the new providers of capital. We should look at the fundamental balance struck between capital and other interests through the medium of the joint-stock, limited liability company, a balance that underpins so much of our industrial and commercial life, but that is rarely subjected to scrutiny.

From abroad, we can learn from the experience of the Swedes with wage-earner investment funds, from the US with esops (employee share ownership plans), from the Germans with co-determination and industrial democracy, from the Spanish with Mondragon. Let no one say that socialists have run out of ideas!

## EMPLOYEE OWNERSHIP

One obvious means of diffusing power and democratising the enterprise is to vest ownership of the enterprise in the workforce. Socialists have always been interested in the possibilities of people working together co-operatively as joint owners of their enterprise, as a means, not just of extending to labour some of the privileges of capital, but of eliminating the separate role of capital altogether. The Labour Party has paid too little attention to these co-operative ideas, preferring over recent years to look to a model of centralised State ownership.

Many socialists have traditionally felt more comfortable with the concept of workers remaining in a position of opposition to the providers of capital. On the other hand, the ideas that workers should, in addition to a fair price for their labour, also have the fruits of their labour returned to them, and that labour should hire capital rather than the other way round, have a long socialist pedigree, and seem increasingly appropriate to modern conditions.

There are still many on the Left who are troubled by the problem that, in many models of employee ownership, the workers do not so much displace the capitalist as become capitalists themselves. There is, it is true, an interesting theoretical argument as to whether employee ownership should be based on the employees' role as the suppliers of labour, or whether the employees should themselves become the suppliers and controllers of capital in the enterprise and derive their rights of ownership from that fact.

In practical terms, it matters little. We should, of course, pay particular attention to the rights that attend the provision of labour as opposed to the provision of capital, but we should not ignore the potential of conflating the two roles, and encouraging workers to take over the capital-providers' role in their own enterprises. To refuse to entertain this possibility would provide an instructive example of the way in which an excessive attachment to dogma can sometimes mislead us into concentrating on too narrow an objective – in this case, the assault on the rights of capital – rather than on the broader and more universally valid socialist objective of diffusing power more widely.

The case for employee ownership rests on both moral and practical considerations. The socialist will support employee ownership on the ground that men and women should have control over their own lives, including their working lives, and should enjoy the fruits of their own labour. This is an important reflection of the socialist concern for individual freedom and fulfilment, and it rests on a concept of individual rights, arising from the fact of citizenship and membership of society, rather than from any utilitarian schema.

We are familiar with the notion that the individual rights of each citizen should be expressed in the political domain in the form of a political democracy through which we delegate rather than surrender our authority to the legislators. The idea is less familiar in the economic sphere.

In the capitalist firm, we surrender rather than delegate our authority to the employers. Decisions are not made in our name but in that of the employer; that is the nature of the employment contract. The employer treats labour as a commodity, which he can dispose of as he wishes. The essence of employee ownership is to reclaim for the workers the power of control over their working lives, and to enable them to delegate rather than surrender that power to professional managers where this is appropriate.

The moral and social case for increased self-determination at work is a powerful one, and it is reinforced by the practical benefits it brings. Increased trust, information flows and motivation are all likely to follow from various forms of worker ownership, boosting the performance of the firms concerned. A 1984 study of 347 companies from the National Centre for Employee Ownership in the USA found that companies with esops generated 46 per cent more jobs and 40 per cent more sales growth than they would have done otherwise.

Worker ownership, if extended across the economy, is also likely to produce wider benefits to the economy as a whole.

Apart from the improved performance of individual worker-owned firms, it is likely to reduce wage conflict, and thus pressures leading to inflation, in the wider economy. It is also arguable that a worker-owned firm, maximising profit per employee, will increase the capital intensity and productivity of the firm to a greater extent than would be true of a conventional capitalist firm.

It must be emphasised that these benefits arise only if the change in ownership is real and is reflected in a changed relationship between managers and others. Thus worker ownership goes beyond profit-related pay, or share schemes, which on their own are likely to have only a marginal effect. The essence of both the moral and practical case for employee ownership is that it effects a real transfer of control.

Many employee share schemes (particularly those supported by some City institutions and many of those established in the United States) do not attempt to achieve this aim. There is, in other words, an essential difference between employee share schemes that do not transfer real power to employees, and those that do. Too often, worker-owners are expected to be 'employees by day and shareholders by night'. Only in employee ownership schemes that accord with socialist criteria is the attempt made to reclaim power for the workforce.

If that is to be achieved, a number of practical questions have to be addressed. Should employees have individual stakes in the firm or in the employee-owned holding company? If they do have individual stakes, should they be obliged to sell their holdings back to the company or a trust? Should they be limited in size? Should employees share in the profits as workers or as shareholders, and should they exercise their right to control as workers or as shareholders? Should there be outside shareholders?

There is no doubt that permitting individual stakes can create problems. On the one hand, retiring workers can, if the company must re-buy their shares, create cash-flow problems and prevent accumulation, while on the other hand, the company will cease to be worker-owned if employees can sell their stakes on the open market. Moreover, workers may take too great a personal risk, if a substantial part of their savings is invested in the same firm that employs them.

These arguments are not, however, decisive. While it is true that the freedom to re-sell on the open market would destroy worker ownership in due course if permitted without limit (as is now threatened at the National Freight Corporation), it is possible to create systems which alleviate the cash-flow and accumulation problems presented by company re-purchase where this is the preferred option. The problem of double jeopardy can also be overcome by permitting workers to invest only a small proportion of their savings and pension rights in the company for which they work.

In addition, positive and persuasive arguments can be made for individual stakes that are re-purchasable by the company or by an employee trust. In many instances, individual stakes are what engage people's attention and enthusiasm; socialists should not be slow to acknowledge the power of self-interest as a motivator and the possibilities of using self-interest to secure public-interest objectives. In many instances, it will be the element of individual involvement and gain that will popularise and give practical effect to employee ownership.

Moreover, it can be argued that without individual stakes, there may be little incentive for corporate saving. Without the prospect of individual capital appreciation, workers may prefer to distribute the whole of the available surplus, rather than re-invest it for the benefit of future generations of workers. The consequence then is either low capital accumulation rates (as experienced by traditional British producer co-ops) or inflationary borrowing to finance investment (as has occurred in Yugoslavia).

It can also be argued that if workers have no interest as individual shareholders, it might be difficult to attract outside equity finance, on the assumption that this is desirable. Without the safeguard of an individual employee stake in the future of the firm (and the consequent recognition of the need for re-investment), the providers of outside equity may not feel that their interests will be adequately protected.

The conclusion should be, therefore, that individual stakes should be permitted in many cases, but that they should not be saleable on the open market, and they should not initially be very large. Special structures will be needed to facilitate re-purchase of the stakes and to ensure that individual stakes are made compatible with collective and democratic control. It is, of course, quite possible to exclude individual stakes from employee ownership schemes, but companies owned in this way will probably remain relatively unimportant.

A related issue is whether the right to share in the profits and to vote should be attached proportionately to shares according to their value or should instead be assigned equally to all employees. It is clearly important that a small group of employees should not own a large and disproportionate block of shares and thus have control. This danger can be avoided if everyone starts with the same stake; even if long-serving employees subsequently acquire larger stakes because of the undistributed profits attributed to their shares, this is unlikely to make such a significant difference as to affect control. The issue becomes one of whether or not long-serving employees should have marginally more say in policy meetings – a detail that does not affect the fundamental principle.

If employee owners are limited in the size of investment they can make, there will be many cases where some form of outside finance will be necessary. This could in principle be limited to debt, rather than taking the form of equity, and there are those who believe that such a limitation is important. It will usually be possible to raise outside equity only if it is given voting rights, and those voting rights would immediately threaten to swamp the workers' votes – precisely the position in conventional capitalist firms with employee share schemes. Moreover, equity earns an unlimited return, which, given that its liability is limited, is unjust. Outside equity finance may in any case be unnecessary, as shown, for example, by the experience of Mondragon.

On the other hand, it can be argued that it is possible to ensure the maintenance of worker control and at the same time create collective structures that protect the interests of outside equity. Outside interests would then be merely a brake on worker decisions, rather than a controlling force. And while it is true that an unlimited return to those with a limited liability may be unjust, there is no reason why this injustice should be neglected only in the case of employee ownership rather than more generally. There may in any case be little that can be done about such injustice in a world of relatively free capital flows –

equity in the balance sheet will usually be necessary in order to secure debt, and only enthusiasts will buy this in a free market if offered a capped return.

As to Mondragon, it has been widely observed that Mondragon has depended on a flow of debt finance that is in turn dependent on community good will and a strong propensity to save. They have, in other words, raised money that UK capital markets would not have supplied. The more general experience must surely be that equity finance is needed.

How is the company to accumulate capital in the long run if it has to buy back the stakes sold to it by departing members? At Mondragon, this problem is met by paying 30 per cent of profits into indivisible reserves, which are never paid out. This could be combined with a high depreciation rate policy, to ensure a steady real accumulation rate. In addition, members' stakes could be converted on leaving, not into cash, but into subordinated annuities or debt.

Many employee-owned enterprises, for all these reasons, will allow individual shareholdings, will pay profits to capital rather than labour, and will permit outside equity. This does not mean, however, that there will not continue to be a place for a 'pure' co-operative sector, subject to more stringent conditions such as those laid down by the Industrial Common Ownership Movement (ICOM), or the International Co-operative Alliance, or the Industrial and Provident Societies Act 1965. These conditions will often suit the individuals and the businesses concerned, and should be encouraged in their own right; support for one form of employee ownership should not exclude the development of others.

There are a number of encouragements the Government could offer, by ensuring that bodies like ICOM and the national network of local co-operative development agencies are adequately funded, and by allowing local authorities to provide advice and assistance. New tax provisions could remove some of the handicaps that co-ops currently suffer, by, for example, allowing them to plough back their earnings into a statutory reserve without becoming liable to corporation tax, and by making sure that co-ops qualify for all the help available to small businesses generally.

Incentives should be provided to encourage firms to become

co-ops by phasing out capital gains and corporation tax liability on conversions, reducing the costs of registration and offering workers the first right of refusal when their firms are threatened by closure. Some of these encouragements could be offered to all forms of worker ownership.

Perhaps more important, Government can and should invest in co-ops and worker-controlled companies. This can be justified by the prejudice shown by capital market institutions against worker-controlled firms, despite the fact that the failure rate for new co-ops is lower than that for conventional companies.

The British economy is unusual in Europe in the relatively small role played by co-ops. In Europe as a whole, the co-operative sector is rightly seen as an important third force – in addition to the public and private sectors – and as a means of creating cost-effective and stable employment, very often for those whose employment prospects are otherwise limited. We should look to a similarly important role for co-ops in Britain.

If worker-owned firms are really to progress, however, they must find ways of ensuring that outside financing remains possible without threatening worker control, that incentives to entrepreneurs are not lost, that management élites do not become entrenched, that democracy within the firm is real, and that the company does not suffer from the excessive risk aversion that has been identified as a characteristic drawback of the worker-owned firm. There is a range of measures to help to create this necessary balance. The most promising of these measures is the esop, or employee share ownership plan.

ESOPS

It is a measure of the extent to which the Labour movement has sometimes allowed its thinking to be tied into a straitjacket that the advocacy of shareholding as a means of securing worker ownership and control has often attracted a somewhat hysterical reaction. This has arisen partly because of a genuine confusion between esops – as an instrument of workers' control – and individual shareholdings as a corollary of privatisation, partly because of a misapprehension that esops were being offered as a substitute for other forms of public ownership rather than as an additional instrument of common ownership, and partly because of an unthinking antipathy to the whole concept of share ownership – a prime example of attaching excessive importance to labels and shying away from ghosts.

The fact is that share ownership will increasingly become a common experience for many people in Britain. If we cut ourselves off from that experience, we shall be repeating the mistake we made over home ownership. Far better to develop a concept and practice of share ownership that serves the socialist interest in diffusing power, rather than the capitalist preoccupation with preserving and concentrating the privileges of capital. The esop offers us the chance of doing exactly that.

Esops are attractive because they create a balance of interest between shareholder and employee, avoid excessive risk aversion, need not entrench management in a harmful way, and deal with the accumulation problem. Esops come in various forms, but always involve an intermediate vehicle, which owns shares in the employing company. Under current legislation, this vehicle is most usefully a trust, of which the employees are beneficiaries, though the principle of the esop would be retained were legislation to encourage the vehicle to be a limited company, with the employees of the employing company as the sole shareholders.

The intermediate vehicle buys an equity stake in the company (either existing shares on the market or new shares from the company). To do this it borrows money, and services and repays the debt out of dividends on the equity stake, plus additional profit-share payments from the employing company.

It is only as the assets of the vehicle increase to exceed its liabilities that there is a distribution of individual stakes to employees. The increase in the value of the assets comes from the profit-share payments but could also arise from an increase in the value of the equity. For as long as the debt remains, the creditor has partial control of the vehicle through, for example, having the right to nominate some of the trustees.

Employees thus have an interest in a certain target profit level being achieved. The threshold for success is raised from break-even to the point at which profit-share payments and rises in the share price allow the debt to be serviced and paid off.

Outside shareholders' interests are protected, so that continuing outside equity funding is encouraged. Excessive risk aversion is avoided. Yet, at the same time, profit maximisation in the interests of outside shareholders is replaced by profit targets set in the interests of the worker-owners.

The problem of entrenched or hostile management can also be overcome. If the employees felt that they were being obstructed by an unsympathetic or otherwise unacceptable management, they could, through the trustees, accept a takeover bid for the vehicle's stake (in return for a stake in the bidder), or invite an alternative management team to fight a proxy battle for board positions. While an agreed bid from another company may serve the interests of the worker-owners, by allowing them to install a new management team, one of the great advantages of the esop is that it creates an obstacle to takeovers if they are regarded as being against the interests of employees.

When employees retire or leave that employment, they sell shares back, not to the employing company but to the vehicle. (This is not a feature of all esops, but is necessary if employee ownership is to continue.) The vehicle borrows to finance this share purchase where necessary, just as it borrowed to purchase the shares originally. The accumulation problem is thus side-stepped.

The borrowing to finance the original share purchase, and any re-purchase, depends on the willingness of the banks to finance the operation. In general, financing the purchase of equity with debt is bad business, but banks will do this in the case of esops, because the company usually gives them a charge on the assets, including those acquired with the proceeds of any new shares issued to the vehicle, and because the fact of employee ownership is generally recognised as minimising any risk.

The beneficiaries of a trust do not have any right to nominate trustees. The terms of an esop can, however, specify that employee beneficiaries elect all or some of the trustees, and the Finance Act 1989 provides that an esop qualifying for 'fast track' tax relief must have a majority of worker trustees. Unity Trust – the trade union financed merchant bank which is the leading force in setting up esops in this country – encourages rules giving all employees one vote in trustee elections. Thus, esops need not but can be encouraged to provide a democratic mechanism from day one, before any individual stakes have been distributed.

Individual stakeholders can also delegate their voting rights in the employing company to the trustees. If esops are to be encouraged, the democratic potential could be developed further – either by altering the relevant trust law, or by altering the tax laws so that the vehicles used tended not to be trusts but companies.

If esops are to succeed – in the sense that they become widely established and carry socialist values into practice – it is essential that they should be 'democratic' esops – that is, esops in which the employee-owners exercise control. Unless the holding is significant, unless the management supports it, and unless genuine participative structures are set up within the company (in addition to the formal rights of workers to elect trustees) raised expectations may be disappointed and the end result may be worse than if nothing had happened at all. This has been the US experience in many cases.

Government can, of course, help in a number of ways. Tax incentives can be offered, though care has to be taken not to encourage esops for the wrong reasons. The legal technicalities can be simplified. Government can buy stakes in companies, use those stakes to ensure the appointment of sympathetic top management and then sell the stakes to esops, as one aspect of the work of an interventionist institution such as the British Technology Enterprise suggested in Labour's Policy Review. This could be done gradually, in an attempt to encourage others to follow the example. At the same time, regional development agencies could be encouraged to play the role of advocate and facilitator, along the lines of New York Governor Cuomo's employee-ownership office.

A further problem is that, even if democratic esops become common, there is plenty of evidence – from America and Yugoslavia – that systems of this type are easily hijacked by management. The danger is that management achieves control both of the trust and of the operating company and then ensures employee apathy and acquiescence in traditional authority.

Trade unions therefore have a key countervailing role to

play. They do not need a right of representation, but they can organise employees to stand for election as trustees. They will also perhaps have to provide services to the trustees and, in particular, the services of executives sufficiently proficient in management and finance to monitor management's perform-ance and to understand what is needed to achieve growing profits.

One of the leading British examples of a successful esop illustrates some of these points. The People's Provincial bus company was established following a failed management buy-out attempt of the municipal passenger transport undertaking in Gosport and Fareham. James Freeman, the acting assistant managing director, led a 100 per cent employee buy-out, of which 80 per cent was achieved through an esop. The original idea had been to set up a co-operative, but the employees were advised that they would find funding easier if they used the esop form.

The esop owns a majority of the shares and is controlled by trustees, some nominated by Barclays and Unity Trust, through whom the buy-out was financed, and some employees elected by their colleagues. The employee-trustees are not union officials – a point emphasised by Alex Hodder, the TGWU official who played a major part in setting up the esop – though they might be lay officials or members and as such 'accountable to the union through their branch'. The company board is thus responsible to the esop trustees.

Week-to-week democracy within the company is ensured through the participation committee, which thrashes out all the major issues, with representatives from all 'constituencies' within the 200-strong company – that is, two each from the NUR and the TGWU, one from clerical, one from engineering, and one from junior management, as well as the senior management.

Each employee was invited to take a £750 initial individual stake held directly, in addition to the esop. This was not compulsory, but 185 out of the 207 employees paid, normally by taking out personal loans. Hodder notes the problem created by new employees; many did not pay the £750 but were then given free shares (by general but not universal agreement). This type of issue will, he fears, create tensions; the rules on membership are not as clear-cut as they might be, so that, for example, there is no requirement that all new employees must join the company.

Hodder makes a number of shrewd points about enterprises such as this. People's Provincial is a relatively low-risk business with a strong asset base and low capital requirements. It was therefore easy to finance externally and perfectly possible to ask for more than token stakes from employees. Moreover, the price at which it was acquired reflected a discount authorised under the appropriate legislation because of the fact that it was an employee buy-out. The company operates in a sector (labour-intensive consumer services) where the fact of employee ownership is a plus with customers; in industrial services and manufacturing, customers might consciously or unconsciously be less enthusiastic about a worker-owned concern. It may be difficult, therefore, to generalise from this example to more risky manufacturing businesses.

Hodder recognises that the presence of outside trustees representing creditors is a very valuable stabilising factor. The interests of the creditors are seen as legitimate, and they focus attention on the need to create a surplus to pay off the loan. Hodder is anxious about the stability of the board of trustees when the loan has been paid off in seven or eight years' time and the company is entirely controlled by trustees answerable to the employees. In particular, how will the board of trustees relate to the participation committee? This will be all the more difficult if the membership question has not been settled in a way that is satisfactory to all, and the problems of pockets of resistance, envy and free-riding are not resolved.

The establishment of an esop was possible only because of the progressive attitude of management, and chiefly of James Freeman. Many managements would not have accepted these arrangements – largely out of antipathy to the idea of an increased role for the workforce.

Hodder warns that the constant danger of apathy and deference can be dealt with only by continuing education on ways of working and monitoring performance. This does mean, of course, a continuing role for trade unions. Despite Hodder's personal involvement and his own role as a full-time union official, there is considerable hesitation in his union about such ventures. Hodder feels that unions must meet this challenge of 'responsibility' and put their wealth of industrial experience to use.

Despite these cautionary points, People's Provincial seems likely to be the forerunner of many more successful esops. The hesitations of the trade unions who, through the Unity Trust bank, have been important proponents of the idea, seem likely to diminish as experience grows and the advantages of esops – often as alternatives to closure or redundancy – become more apparent. The Labour movement as a whole should be clear that worker ownership in this form is a valuable means of achieving the socialist aim of diffusing power.

CHANGES IN COMPANY LAW AND INDUSTRIAL DEMOCRACY

The limited liability company is an extraordinary institute, whose peculiarities are so familiar to us that they pass virtually unnoticed. The doctrine of limited liability means that the providers of capital to an enterprise enjoy, in addition to the ordinary rights of ownership, which they exercise to the exclusion of others, the right to leave debts unpaid if the enterprise should fail.

The case for limited liability is, of course, a strong one. It is the means by which people and institutions are induced to provide capital to enterprises over whose management and direction they have very little individual control. Without the privilege of limited liability, investors would be reluctant to entrust their capital to managers who are largely unknown to them. Limited liability has therefore been of crucial importance in stimulating the supply of capital that has financed industrial expansion and underpinned rising living standards.

It is nevertheless hard to see why the providers of capital should enjoy, in addition to the limited liability which is necessary to induce them to invest, all the other powers of ownership. They have, collectively, the exclusive rights of ownership; this means that people or institutions who may have little connection with or interest in an enterprise, other than the fact that they have bought pieces of paper, have the power to decide policy, hire and fire, buy and sell, take the profits – all to the exclusion of others who may devote their working lives to the enterprise or provide the custom that keeps the enterprise alive.

Employees are limited to the remuneration and the employment rights provided under their contracts of employment (as supplemented, on some issues, by employment law). Consumers receive only the goods or services they contract to pay for, and have only limited rights of redress against and influence over the enterprise. The shareholder alone has the rights of control, and the right to take the profits – a right to unlimited profits, it should be noted, which is hard to square with the limited liability they enjoy.

It is hard to see why the principle of limited liability should require this panoply of exclusive ownership rights for shareholders when most investors are attracted by the limitation of liability, rather than any other aspect of ownership. This point is reinforced by the fact that, in practice, shareholders do not seem very interested in the additional rights of ownership, and in many cases the rights are simply not exercised effectively by anyone.

There is therefore a powerful case, on grounds of equity and efficiency, for redressing the balance between the largely unexercised rights provided to shareholders and the powerlessness suffered by those who are much more intimately connected with or dependent upon the enterprise. It is for this reason that socialists in other countries have paid considerable attention to the possibility of changing company law for this purpose.

The changes so far proposed or implemented have concentrated on questions of representation for workers on company boards, the creation of a new 'membership' status for employees and possibly consumers, the provision of much greater information to employees about company affairs, and the limitation of the return to shareholders to match the limitation of their liability.

The case for industrial democracy, like that for employee ownership, rests on arguments for democracy, employee satisfaction and greater efficiency. Unlike particular forms of ownership, however, which may be appropriate only in certain limited instances, industrial democracy offers an across-the-board reform that will diffuse power and enhance freedom and autonomy.

Industrial democracy offers participation and consultation rather than ownership or control, and it is arguable that, in many instances, this is precisely the level of involvement that is wanted by the workforce. As Lord McCarthy says in a recent Fabian pamphlet: 'The workers generally do not deem it desirable or feasible that they should run the organisation. They merely feel they should be strongly involved in the decision-making processes that affect their work and livelihood.'

The message that industrial democracy can lead to better economic performance has been taken to heart in a number of Western European countries whose economic records are rather better than ours. Worker participation has been legally (though variously) enforced in Sweden, Norway, the Netherlands, Austria and West Germany – and is generally regarded as having improved efficiency in those economies.

Industrial democracy will usually be applied in three main areas: information, consultation, and joint decision-taking. In virtually all Western European countries, works councils are established at plant level and above, and are entitled to a full picture of the firm's position. Commercial confidentiality cannot be used as a blanket reason for non-disclosure; appeals can be made to an appeal body if there is any dispute regarding disclosure.

There is also a general duty to consult on issues affecting workers, plus a specific duty to consult on matters such as manpower plans, welfare, pensions and so on. An issue on which consultation would be of particular importance to British workforces is that of proposed merger or takeover. It is one of the most marked and unacceptable features of the takeover activity we have witnessed over recent years that it has been the workforces, whose interests are often the most directly affected, who are the last to know what is happening. A change in the law, so as to provide specific statutory rights to workers, is long overdue.

Joint decision-making, which is both the most far-reaching and also the most controversial area, is something of which we have only a limited and somewhat unsatisfactory experience in this country. The recommendation in the Bullock Report that there should be worker representation on the board was applied in modified form in the Post Office, but only for two years and with little impact, substantially because management resented it and fought against it. More limited co-determination at lower levels – normally about 'social matters' (as in West Germany) – works more smoothly.

Rather more far-reaching is the proposal that the company should not comprise just its shareholders but should have 'members' who would include employees as well as shareholders. This would substantially change the nature of the company. The major effect would be, by virtue of providing voting rights to employee-members, to extend the powers of decision-making beyond the ranks of the providers of capital and to enfranchise the workers, not just in a political but in an economic sense.

The members would, by virtue of their voting rights, be able to insist on representation and accountability without the burden of day-to-day supervision and control. Financial benefits to the new classes of members might or might not be included. In principle, membership could be extended to other groups, such as consumers, although the problems of defining the appropriate nexus in such cases would become increasingly difficult.

A further variation on the theme of changing the respective rights of capital and labour in the company is the proposal that, rather than extend to the workforce some of the rights of shareholders, the shareholders should have their rights limited, to reflect the privilege of limited liability which they enjoy. There is much to be said in equity for such a proposal. The difficulty is that, if such a change were not universal, so that the suppliers of capital retained a choice as to whether to invest in companies offering them an unlimited or a limited return, they would in most cases opt for the unlimited return; and, in a world of free capital movements, even compulsion within the British context would not remove that choice from them.

It may be better therefore – in the cases of proposals for both what might be called 'membership' and 'limited return' companies – to recognise that compulsion is unlikely to succeed. The better course is to offer clear rules for those who wish to make such changes, and perhaps tax and other incentives to encourage companies to adopt these more enlightened and forward-looking forms of company status. We should aim at a growing sector of these 'socially owned' companies, whose success in both the commercial and social spheres would encourage others to adopt the same course.

## PENSION FUNDS

In seeking the means of dispersing power and increasing democracy, we should not overlook the potential of existing institutions. Of these, by far the most significant are the pension funds. Pension funds, which are merely the collected savings of millions of ordinary people, have become by far the most important source of capital for the stock market. They already provide a large proportion of new equity capital, and by the turn of the century will own a majority of British industry.

There is here, therefore, an immense potential for effective social ownership. The substance is already there. The principle – that the providers of capital should be entitled to powers of ownership and control – can hardly be disputed by the apologists for capitalism. All that is needed to make pension funds a powerful instrument of social ownership is some relatively minor changes in rules and practice.

At present, pension funds are usually run as trusts, to which the law of private trusts is applicable. This private law element remains strongly entrenched. Most occupational pension schemes depend entirely on the terms of the trust deed, and there is remarkably little statutory intervention. The law of trusts was developed by equity judges to allow wealthy individuals to dispose of their property in ways that allowed them to retain control of it beyond their deaths and – increasingly in recent decades – to minimise liability to tax. It is hardly the ideal means of regulating major sources of investment capital in a modern industrial economy.

Pension funds are legally owned by trustees appointed for the purpose and in whom the property (the contributions) is vested by the trust deed. The trustees are answerable in legal terms to the beneficial owners, but the powers of control exercised by the beneficiaries are very limited. They can sue the trustees for any breach of fiduciary duty, but have little say in matters of day-to-day administration.

In practice, the trustees carry out their duties by employing professional fund managers or – more usually – by contractually delegating the administration of the fund to a firm of investment managers. As a consequence, what could be a powerful expression of the investment power of millions of small savers ends up instead in the hands of a handful of investment managers in the City.

The trustees and the professional managers are in turn constrained by the requirements of trust law. Their discretion is limited by the obligation to act in the interests of the beneficiaries, and this is narrowly interpreted to mean that they must invest in such a way as to produce the best return commensurate with the safety of the investment. Hence, the trustees would not find it easy to take into consideration factors other than immediate accounting criteria. They could not easily give expression to political objectives, such as the wider public or national interest, or avoid certain investments merely because they disapproved of them on political grounds, or give priority to particular investments such as investment in their own locality or region.

Any effective dispersion of power through pension funds must therefore involve two stages – the transfer of control of pension funds to employee representatives and the active use of that control freed from the restrictions of the current law. These changes should benefit the fund beneficiaries, but also the fund's finances in the long term.

Beneficiaries should be given the right to vote for trustees. Employee representatives will need training on the implications of control. The already existing Pensions and Investment Resource Centre could be built up as a source of information for all those wishing to exercise responsibility. Legal changes may help here – in particular, a further extension of the information fund managers are obliged to provide, and which the trustees are obliged to pass on to members.

## WAGE-EARNER FUNDS

One of the most interesting measures to extend ownership and control of industry to a wider section of the population has been the Swedish experiment with wage-earner funds. The experiment was introduced in 1983, and has now run for long enough to allow us to make some judgment of its effects.

The original proposals made by the Swedish LO (the Swedish TUC) in 1976 were for something like compulsory esops. This provoked violent controversy, however, and what was enacted in 1983 was a significantly watered-down version of the original idea. Nevertheless, the objectives originally set out in the 1976 proposal continue to underpin the exercise.

Those objectives were to facilitate the wage policy of solidarity, so that all workers, and not just those in the most successful firms, shared in increasing prosperity; to counter-act the concentration of power and wealth that would otherwise occur; to increase worker control in industry; to increase capital formation; and to strengthen the pension system. These objectives were to be achieved by enabling workers to share in profits, other than through wage increments, in a collective form that also brought them some degree of control over industry.

The 1983 legislation set up five employee investment funds on a regional basis, but with more limited scope than had originally been proposed. The funds were established on a provisional basis for an experimental period of seven years, and were restricted in the proportion of equity they could hold in any particular enterprise.

The rules actually create a scheme that is closer to a democratic State pension scheme financed out of profits than anything else. In Britain, we have no need for the wage-earner funds in their Swedish form, since we already have a fully developed scheme of occupational pensions, and the pension funds already have a far more important investment role than the wage-earner funds are allowed to have under the Swedish rules.

The question for us, however, is whether we can take some of the essential characteristics of the wage-earner funds and incorporate them in our existing pension funds. The wage-earner funds have a public investment function and duty and are consciously organised on a regional basis; our pension funds do not, and operate entirely in their own narrowly defined interests. The wage-earner funds are deliberately established with substantial worker control; the pension funds are in practice run by professional fund managers, with little real accountability to the worker beneficiaries.

The wage-earner funds are financed in such a way as to reduce excess profits and to maintain wage-earners' solidarity by sharing the benefits of profitability; the pension funds are linked exclusively to the contributions made by the employers and employees of the particular company. The wage-earner funds are the exclusive property of the workers; the pension funds are often treated as a company asset.

The lesson we should draw from the wage-earner funds is therefore not so much that we should seek to replicate them exactly, but that there are important objectives that the Swedes think it worthwhile to seek to achieve in this way, and that we could usefully seek to incorporate in our own institutions. They should, in other words, act as a spur to reforming and extending the role of institutions like the pension funds, and should act as antidote to faint-hearts who argue that nothing other than the accountant's advice must be allowed to influence investment decisions.

## REGIONAL ENTERPRISE BOARDS

One of the most encouraging developments in recent years, during a period of economic difficulty – particularly in the regions – and of assaults on the independence of local government, has been the success of regional enterprise boards. They have developed partly as an alternative to competitive regional promotion, as a response to unemployment. They were designed to plug the gap in the capital market's provision of long-term development capital, particularly in those relatively small parcels that City-based venture capital firms find it uneconomic to assess and monitor. In addition, by establishing the viability of investment in their regions by their own example, they help to attract further funds to those regions.

Regional enterprise boards enjoy the advantages of local knowledge and commitment, plus lower costs than those of City firms. As a result, they appear to have achieved their objectives, albeit on a relatively small scale. The five 'first wave' boards – West Midlands, West Yorkshire, Merseyside, Lancashire and Greater London – had by the end of 1986 invested £35m in 200 companies, creating or sustaining 14,000 jobs. Total investment by regional enterprise boards is now £75 million. Most important, they have been able to lever private capital into their regions – between £2 and £4 for every £1 of local authority money – and the West Midlands Enterprise Board (with Lazards) and Merseyside (with local businessmen) have set up regional unit trusts.

They operate much like venture capital firms, appointing non-executive directors and setting up agreements about the information to be provided. They often stipulate employment practices; Merseyside, for example, encourages trade union involvement. They also offer various development services, including training (such as Lancashire's courses for female engineers, cross-subsidised by investment profits), premises, sectoral research and consultancy, and technology transfer. Most see part of their role as promoting good employment practices and assisting disadvantaged groups. Some specialise in manufacturing and services to manufacturing.

A further development of enterprise board work is 'institutional entrepreneurship'. Job Ownership Limited has reported on this as undertaken at Mondragon and has suggested the formation of a British unit. The objective is to create new employment – replacing pure entrepreneurship with what would operate like the new ventures department of a large company – with the difference that it would allow independent or semi-independent ventures, including co-ops, and would, of course, require that the new employment should be in the desired region. Enterprise remains individual – but the backing and support service comes through local institutions rather than the organisational hierarchy of large firms.

The concept of municipal enterprise and ownership has much to commend it. A new Labour Government should not only look to the enterprise boards to play a larger role; it should also free them and their local authority backers from the constraints that the Tory Government has imposed upon them. Local authorities should be given a wider and more general competence to raise money and to use resources to take a more active role in the promotion of local and regional enterprise.

# CHAPTER EIGHT

# *Empowering the Consumer*

## THE IMPORTANCE OF CONSUMPTION

The socialist project can be powerfully advanced by diffusing economic power amongst employees and producers. Not everyone is, however, a producer. While the producer's role is important, an exclusive emphasis on the producer will overlook the fact that the consumer is in some senses even more important – because consumption in the widest sense is the end objective of economic activity – and that we all are consumers.

Socialists have tended in the past to disregard the consumer. This has partly been because of the Marxist emphasis on the differing economic roles of capital and labour in the process of production, partly because of the role of the trade unions as producerist organisations, partly because of an old-fashioned labourist and anti-employer sentiment, and – perhaps most important – because in past times, and before consumption became as complex and laden with both choice and danger as it is today, consumption as a function did not seem to be a separate activity of any importance.

This insensitivity to the role of consumption has handicapped us very substantially in the task of adapting to and recognising the higher standards of choice and quality that are now demanded by consumers, whose increased purchasing power has given them a new economic power and who have, in a very real sense, been enfranchised as a consequence.

An exclusive attention paid to the interests of producers has encouraged us to overlook these new demands and aspirations, and has allowed our opponents to wrong-foot us. Yet it is our opponents who ought to be on the defensive, since it is they who champion the power of the monopoly producer and the exploitation of the consumer, and it is they who are indifferent to the relative impotence of some consumers in relation to others. These are opportunities for the socialist to exploit.

REGULATING THE UTILITIES

It is inevitable and to a large extent desirable that much of the provision on which the consumer depends will be undertaken in one shape or form by the market. As we have already seen, this necessitates a readiness to intervene, in order to prevent abuses of market power and to equalise to some extent the power of the consumer, in relation both to the producer and to other consumers. There are, however, some special problems that should be considered.

The major utilities are, as we have seen, natural monopolies, whatever their form of ownership. While efforts can and should be made to introduce competition where appropriate, the nature of the undertaking will in most cases mean that the consumer has no alternative supplier to turn to if he or she is dissatisfied with the service provided.

As a consequence, and irrespective of the form of ownership, the utilities pose a threat as monopolies to the consumer interest. The problem is, of course, more acute if the undertaking is in private ownership, since the consumer interest will struggle to have any influence in the face of the drive for shareholders' profit; but even in public ownership, it is all too easy for the enterprise to become almost exclusively producer-oriented and for the consumer interest to be overlooked.

The solution is to recognise that the special responsibilities and monopoly position of the utilities require a special regime, whether they are publicly or privately owned. That regime should take the form of a regulatory framework that takes account of the fact that the utilities are enterprises of special public interest.

Regulatory commissions should be established for each enterprise. The commissions should be appointed by Government but should be set up with statutory powers providing maximum independence, both of Government and of the industry to be regulated. The consumer and trade union interest should be specifically represented in the membership of the commission.

Their function would be to establish, as a result of consultation with the enterprise and in the light of the national and consumer interest, standards of service, maximum prices, investment levels and so on. Matters of a wider import – such as environmental behaviour, non-discriminatory policies, employee consultation and participation – could also be prescribed and monitored. Sanctions in the form of financial penalties and powers to replace senior management and board members would be applied in the case of failure to meet prescribed targets.

The commission would also require the maximum disclosure of information to both employees and consumers. It should conduct hearings in public at which consumers and other interests could give evidence and make submissions. It would make regular reports to Parliament.

The commission would be responsible for dealing with consumer complaints and would offer both a forum in which general complaints and issues could be dealt with, and a system of redress for individual breaches of the duty to achieve customer satisfaction.

This system of regulation, which is closely based on the US experience, would do more to meet the major problem arising from monopoly – the powerlessness of the consumer – than any other measure. It would help to create a consumer-oriented ethos in all the major utilities and would divert us from the misleading notion that the problem can be met simply through changes in ownership. It would have the additional advantage, in the case of privately owned utilities, of powerfully introducing the notion of the public interest into the private sector.

Ownership would, of course, continue to be crucial where the public interest demanded more than mere regulation, as where, for example, major investment programmes were required, which could be financed only from the public purse. It has to be recognised, too, that regulation is likely to be difficult when the regulator has insufficient information, or is personally committed to the interests of the producer, or is directed to fix prices on the basis of formulae, such as rate of return maxima, that largely ignore the consumer interest and create perverse reactions, such as cost increases and under-investment, or when anti-competitive behaviour is difficult to detect.

## MAINTAINING MARKET COMPETITION

The problem of regulating the major utilities is just one aspect of a wider problem – that of preventing the natural tendency of markets to create monopolies and consequently to disadvantage the consumer in relation to the producer. In the case of the utilities, their status as natural monopolies leads to solutions based on common or social ownership and strict regulation; even here, however, some attention should be paid to the structure of the industry, and every opportunity should be taken, consistent with the basic purposes and performance of the utility concerned, to introduce competition wherever possible – both in the form of outside competitors and of internally organised competition and decentralisation.

The wider problem, however, goes well beyond the realm of the utilities. It involves the whole ambit of what might be called competition and anti-trust policy. It is a field to which British socialists, given our theoretical critique of the market's tendency towards monopoly, have devoted surprisingly little practical attention.

A positive interventionist policy to deal with restrictive practices, market abuse and monopoly should be a cardinal element of any socialist policy, on the basic socialist principle of resisting and counter-acting any concentration of power. British policy has traditionally taken too narrow and legalistic a view of these matters, looking to form rather than substance, and wrongly eschewing any general principle that would outlaw uncompetitive practices. There would be great advantage in adopting as the basis of our law the sort of general principle concerning abuse of market power that is embodied in Article 85 of the Treaty of Rome, and in borrowing from the Americans the anti-trust laws that enable them to compel the break-up of concentrations of industrial and market power. The dominant theme should be, in other words, a readiness to respond to an abuse of market power whenever it occurs and whatever form it might take, rather than concentrating as we do at present on form alone.

The problem presents itself in more specific form when it comes to mergers and takeovers. This issue is particularly pressing for the British economy because of the already concentrated and centralised nature of British industrial ownership and the immense amount of takeover activity we experience; the value of the assets involved in bids in recent years exceeds, for example, the budget for health care in this country.

There is also the peculiarly open nature of the British market for corporate control. Most British companies have little protection against hostile takeover. Provided the predator can offer an attractive enough deal to the shareholders, the company will change hands, whatever the preferences of the workforce and the existing directors – another striking example of the immense privileges accorded to capital. In other countries, such as West Germany, the structure of industry – based as it often is on a close nexus between industry, the banks and State institutions – is much more difficult to penetrate, and hostile bids have much less chance of success.

There is little evidence that the high degree of takeover activity in Britain is to the advantage of the national economy. Indeed, the academic evidence strongly suggests that the national economy suffers, as do the parties to mergers and takeovers – to say nothing of the employees. Merger activity reinforces the short-termism of decision-making in British industry, acting not only on those directly involved, but constantly posing the threat of hostile bids to every boardroom in the country.

A high level of takeover activity is the symptom of an economy that is functioning badly rather than well. It signifies an economy in which corporate progress is made, not through investment in new productive capacity, innovation and greater competitiveness, but through increasing market share by acquisition and by eliminating competitors.

For all these reasons, we should take a much tougher approach to mergers and takeovers, and should not shy away from placing considerable obstacles in their way. We should, for example, reverse the burden of proof, so that it is for the parties (or the bidder, in the case of a hostile bid) to show that the bid is in the public interest. The presumption that such a bid is not in the public interest should be reinforced whenever one or more of a number of specific factors – a threat to employment, regional balance and autonomy or national strategic interests, the likelihood of asset-stripping (as evidenced, for example, by a high degree of leveraging), the lack of reciprocity in the case of a foreign bid, as well as the threat of anti-competitive behaviour – is identified.

The purpose of this tougher regime is, of course, to prevent a concentration of market power from harming the consumer or the national interest. In addition, the rights of employees, which are almost entirely overlooked in the present law, should be recognised by providing a statutory right to information and consultation. Employees would also benefit, of course, from the measures proposed above to increase their powers of control over the enterprises for which they work.

CONSUMER OWNERSHIP

One way to protect the consumer is for the consumers to own the producer. The prime example of a consumer-owned producer is the Co-op. There are 8·5 million members of consumer co-ops, although only about 30,000 of these are active members. The movement has a turnover of over £4 billion, which makes it a very significant retailer.

At present, however, the relative inefficiency of co-ops, whose market share has halved over the last thirty years, has ended the dividend and limited any special attraction that membership or shopping at the Co-op might have offered. The retail movement's reaction to competition has been imitation rather than innovation; although strenuous efforts are now being made to improve efficiency and consumer service, little attention seems to be paid to the special attraction the co-operative ethos might offer to customers and members. One innovative bright spot has been the Co-op Bank; it was the first bank to introduce free banking and has set the pace for the competition in a number of ways.

Given this somewhat disappointing record, what is the

potential of the consumer co-operative and how can it be realised? There is still considerable life and merit in the idea of consumer co-ops, and socialists should be keen to develop their operation. The way forward is surely to build positively on the co-op's role as a specifically consumers' organisation, so that, in addition to a level of efficiency that matches that of conventional retailers, the customer is offered a service that is geared to specific consumer needs and interests – the special needs of the disadvantaged or minority groups, and the possibility of asking consumers to decide whether they want products of a particular type or from a particular source.

Membership of the co-op could be much more positively exploited, with members being offered a range of additional facilities, such as travel and social clubs. Members could be more directly involved in the design of services. The co-ops could also extend the idea of forming partnerships with local authorities and trade unions for particular purposes, as in the case of Unity Trust, the merchant bank.

Government can support these developments by recognising the special needs and advantages of consumer co-ops. Because of their interdependent structure, they might need, for example, special exemptions from the restrictive practices legislation, so that retail co-ops can organise wholesale provision.

CREDIT UNIONS

Co-operative ownership has often taken the form of friendly and provident societies of various sorts. One of the most interesting forms is the credit union, a type of mutual savings and investment society, which in other countries, and particularly in West Germany, France and North America, has prompted the development of some of their most important and valuable financial institutions.

The credit union counters the market power of the pawn-broker and loan shark by making use of the community connection. It consists of a group of people with a 'common bond' – such as membership of the same church or club, residents on the same housing estate, employees of the same company – who between them operate a saving and lending operation. Members must save with the union for a given period before they can borrow. The maximum APR they are allowed by law to charge is at present 12·68 per cent, as against the thrift cheque firms' 50 per cent and rates of up to 1000 per cent reported as being charged by loan sharks in some urban areas.

They have not yet, however, taken off in this country. Here, there are only just over eighty operating credit unions, with a total membership of some 34,000 members controlling about £10 million in assets. The average membership is only 335. Yet the need for credit unions has never been greater; over 40 per cent of the adult population remain unbanked, while at the same time the average family indebtedness has for the first time exceeded the average family savings.

The point of credit unions is twofold: they provide cheap credit to those, such as ethnic minorities and those living in the inner cities, who are unattractive to the banks but whose credit-worthiness can be established by their saving record and membership of the 'common bond'; and they provide a financial education to those involved, boosting grass-roots confidence and helping to maintain and develop the community. They might also provide the basis for regionally developed financial institutions, which would retain a regional control of locally generated savings and thereby help to strengthen the regional economy.

Credit unions are potentially a valuable expression of the socialist ideal – of people acting collectively to control their own financial affairs and to strengthen their own community. A Labour Government should provide help and encouragement, and should also raise the current restrictions which limit the level of savings and borrowings.

COMMUNITY BUSINESSES

Community businesses are set up by local residents, often inhabitants of a cluster of streets, to provide local services and jobs (and to make use of Manpower Services Commission (MSC) funds). They started as a reaction to unresponsive local authorities, but have since broadened their activities. They are supported by their local councils but depend heavily on the energy of local inhabitants. The prevailing ethos is one of community benefit rather than self-interest.

The largest network of community businesses is centred on Clydeside, but there are other networks in Scotland and increasingly in England. In Barrowfield, for example, a depressed housing estate in Glasgow with up to 80 per cent unemployment, a community business – a charitable holding company with various operating subsidiaries – has been set up. Operations include a security company, which started by patrolling the estate for the council (and so saving the council money on repairs) and which now has a number of private contracts outside the estate as well; a welding company, mostly working on environmental improvement for the council and which now has its own fabrication unit on the estate; and a painting division, which works for the authority and private businesses. Training and an umbrella support organisation called 'Strathclyde Community Business Limited' are important ingredients.

## PROTECTING THE CONSUMER

A major protection for consumers is the provision of information. The extent to which we currently fall short of keeping the consumer properly informed was graphically illustrated by the gyrations of the Ministry of Agriculture over the salmonella and listeria scares at the end of 1988.

Much progress has, of course, been made since the 1960s in terms of consumer protection legislation, but standards in this country are still not high enough, especially in matters like food labelling. The Consumers Association is inclined to blame the sponsorship role of the Ministry of Agriculture for the poor standards of labelling, and the absence of common standards for the use of names and of clear definitions of words like 'organic' and 'natural'. The Food and Drugs Administration (FDA) in the USA by contrast operates independently of sponsoring ministries and is open in its operations. Possibly as a consequence, standards of labelling are much higher in the USA.

The consumer also needs adequate rights of redress. This is partly a matter of the need to secure changes in substantive law (where, for example, a statutory right of reply against the Press and the broadcasting media is an important reform) and partly a matter of improving access to remedies. Access to the law is in general scandalously too expensive and forbidding; legal remedies are too slow and often inadequate.

We need substantial reforms of the legal system and of legal aid if the law is to serve its proper function. The small claims court procedure appears to work well, though the upper limit on claims should be raised substantially. Crown immunity should be withdrawn from all State undertakings, as has recently been done in the case of hygiene standards in hospitals. Complaints procedures, as in the case of the police, should be made truly independent.

The provision of ombudsman-type remedies, with their relative informality and speed, is an important step forward. The provision of ombudsmen on a voluntary basis by the banking and insurance industries, for example, is to be welcomed. Other professional bodies, such as the Law Society, should follow suit.

We could also learn from the Swedish use of a consumer ombudsman. This official is primarily concerned with misleading sales information (advertising, brochures etc.) and with 'improper terms' in contracts. The public can complain directly to the ombudsman's office; there is also a systematic review of Press advertising and trade association codes as well as random checks.

Local authorities should be encouraged, with new resources and legal powers, to carry out the tasks of setting, monitoring and enforcing consumer standards, and providing appropriate remedies. The individual consumer needs the protection of the law in this way if the overwhelming power of the producer is to be effectively countered.

MAKING COLLECTIVE PROVISION MORE RESPONSIVE

Socialists have traditionally believed in collective provision – the provision of goods and services on an organised, non-market basis, usually by some form of public authority – partly because it is in practical terms the means by which a lack of power in the market can be made good for many people, and partly because it reflects the value that socialists place on the virtues of co-operation as opposed to individual competition. We have not always, however, thought through the case for collective provision in modern circumstances, with the consequence that we have allowed collective provision to be associated too often in the public mind with bureaucracy, imposition and lack of choice.

The case for collective provision is a complex one. In the case of public goods it is essential, because, since we all benefit from them whether or not we pay for them, they are goods that will not be provided by individual effort. There is also the point that the provision of some private goods and services, as in the case of immunisation, confers benefits on those other than the direct recipients, and this requires us to treat these private goods as though they were public.

The collective provision of private goods, on the other hand, is to be justified on different grounds – as one component of community responsibility for basic services; as such it is justified, together with income support, by arguments for equality and economic efficiency. In the absence of collective provision, many people will lack the power in the market to be able to guarantee provision of what may be private but nevertheless essential goods. While one obvious response to this problem will be the attempt to equalise market power through income support, income redistribution, better information and so on, there will be many cases where collective provision is the most appropriate answer. This will be the case, for example, where the service is of fundamental importance both to individuals and to the community – as in the case of education – or where users necessarily have insufficient information to make properly informed decisions in the market – as with health care – or where individuals cannot be allowed to make decisions for dependents.

However strong the case for collective provision, and however central to the socialist project it may be, it must nevertheless meet the only test that matters – whether or not it delivers to individual people the goods and services which they expect and to which they are entitled. Socialists have sometimes been so preoccupied with the collective principle and the collective nature of the provision that they have shied away from facing this simple point. It is almost as though the recognition that it is and can only be individuals who are the end consumers of any provision – collective or not – is regarded as a betrayal of the collective principle. This is a prime example of the way in which a distorted ideology can lead to avoidable errors in practical politics.

There has also been a tendency to concentrate on the interests of the providers, to the exclusion of those of the consumers. Local authorities have sometimes shown more concern for the interests of their employees than for the level of satisfaction with the services provided of those for whom they are intended – though there are welcome signs that this is now changing.

It is therefore very important for the efficacy and acceptability of the principle of collective provision that the consumers of the services should be recognised as the most important people. One way of doing this is to ensure that consumers should have more say in the way in which services are provided. If a service can be designed so that the consumer is offered a genuine choice, which he or she can exercise competently – as, for example, whether women patients would prefer women doctors – then that choice should be offered. We should not be misled into thinking that the market is the only mechanism that provides choice; choice must be consciously built into collective provision.

Individual choice within collective provision can be achieved by paying a subsidy, either direct to the consumer, as in the case of vouchers, or to the producer on the basis of consumption decisions made by the consumers, as in the case of GPs' capitation fees, or payments to private old people's homes. The mechanisms are quite straightforward; the problems arise over whether consumers can make genuine, competent choices, over whether the possibility of choice creates adequate incentives for producers to be responsive, and over whether the results are higher standards for the least advantaged or only for those in privileged positions.

In the NHS, patients already have the right to choose their GP, who is paid on a capitation basis; the market mechanism is already in operation here. However, this right is rarely exercised effectively because there is some reluctance to 'poach' other doctors' patients, because there is a shortage of published information on which patients can base their choice, and because of the relatively small number of practices in any given area.

Accountability on a collective basis may therefore offer in some cases better possibilities than accountability to the individual through the market. If this is to be effective, however, more attention needs to be paid to democratic structures and mechanisms. In the case of health care, for instance, the democratic mechanisms that notionally control the service are entirely unspecific to the NHS. At the national level, it is impossible to express one's preference for the resources to be devoted to health, except by voting for the entire Labour or Conservative programmes. At the regional and district levels, democracy is even more limited; it is impossible, for example, to cast a vote in favour of large centralised hospitals as opposed to small 'community' hospitals, or vice versa.

A hypothecated health tax has been proposed as a means of making democratic control more specific. It is easy to conceive – though no doubt it would be difficult to administer – that such a tax might be levied by an independently elected NHS Board. Elections to such a body would probably command a high turn-out, since they would offer people a chance to influence something of direct concern to themselves.

There may also be an increased role for the Community Health Council (CHC), even though they are not directly representative. CHCs could become the agents of the consumers with an obligation to conduct consumer surveys, and then to act upon them. They would be able to draw on the expertise of organisations representing particular categories of consumers (such as Mind and Age Concern). CHCs of this type would clearly need serious funding and expertise. In the past, both they and the local authority/health authority joint planning process have been weak in the face of the expert power of the medics. The well-known danger, of course, is that as the expertise of the monitoring body grows, it begins to share the professional interests of the service it is monitoring, and is captured. The experience we have of Oftel so far suggests this is not inevitable, but it also shows that freedom of information is essential to enable the monitoring body to do its job properly.

A key factor in monitoring would be performance measurement data, concerned with the quality of the service as well as with economic performance, the terms of which the CHCs would need to control. At present in the health service there is very little performance measurement at all – either of consultants or of hospitals. Data about mortality rates, for example, are rarely made available, though there can be dramatic variations. The right of the public to information would be one important check on the system of goal-setting just described. Another could be nationally determined, enforceable, personal medical rights – which might go beyond the right to a GP and extend, for example, to the right to hospital treatment for certain conditions within a certain period.

Similar considerations apply to other public services. In the case of local authority services, user control has been quite successful in specific areas – leisure facilities, community centres and play facilities, for example. Successful participation of this kind normally involves offering some degree of budget control, and involvement in all stages from planning to feedback, but there is no need for the degree of expertise or technical information required for control of medical provision. In Scandinavia, there are proposals for taking the process a step further, with the allocation of a State-funded budget delegated to committees of users and employees of schools, housing, health clinics and so on.

Where consumers are able to exercise a choice, whether individually or collectively, producers may be forced to become more responsive and to adopt new structures that would make this possible. For example, decentralised housing offices may be forced upon housing departments by tenants' associations, which have the right to employ outside maintenance organisations or do the work themselves if they are dissatisfied. Certain consumers may, however, be unable to make choices either collectively or individually – for example, elderly recipients of various social and medical services. In such cases, managerial initiatives must themselves be the mechanism that leads to greater responsiveness.

A well-documented example of such an initiative is the Kent Community Care Scheme. Under this scheme, case managers were appointed to attend to the needs of a number of elderly people. Each case manager was given a budget, which could be spent on various social services, or as the case manager saw fit. The budget was not integrated with an NHS budget, but it could, for example, have been integrated with a large general practice.

This independent budget control was a key element in motivating the case managers, who were able to define the needs with their clients, and then devise solutions achievable within the budget. Thus it became clear that the clients did not just need food – they needed all the rituals associated with food. It was therefore preferable in some cases not to buy in the meals on wheels service, but to spend the money on helpers who would prepare the meal with the client.

In general, the scheme was a success; old people were more likely to stay in their own home than to move to an old people's home; interviews revealed a higher subjective well-being than before the project; and client's relatives also found it less stressful. The scheme cost less or a monthly basis, though higher survival rates led to slightly increased total expenditure.

Very similar decentralisation measures are taking place in housing departments, and, of course, in the commercial world. Locality planning around the needs of communities of about 15,000 people has been conducted in the Devon Health Service. In general, it is difficult to see why a public service ethic based on decentralisation and responsiveness could not be developed. Martin Smith in a recent Fabian leaflet cites improvements in the service offered by Sheffield, Glasgow and Basildon as examples of increased public sector responsiveness and efficiency resulting from internal initiatives.

# CHAPTER NINE

# Diffusing Political Power

IS DEMOCRACY ENOUGH?

The power which socialists are concerned with and which they want to see widely diffused is, in the end, the power to make choices. It is that power which is the pre-condition and constituent of freedom. It depends partly on a collection of social and economic rights and entitlements, and partly on an assurance that the political system is responsive to each individual.

We are inclined to take it for granted that, because we are a democracy, there is nothing more to be said on the question of political power. Universal suffrage, regular elections, the power to replace one elected Government with another are certainly all present in Britain, and are the essentials of a socialist and democratic diffusion of political power. In the end, nothing in political arrangements matters as much as these basic powers. It has been a fundamental part of the socialist project to see these rights and freedoms established.

We do not need to devalue these achievements in any way in order to say, however, that they may not by themselves fully meet the modern requirements for the diffusion of political power. A vote every four to five years to elect the Government is the foundation-stone, but is the rest of the structure properly designed and constructed?

Are we sure that all the powers and functions that matter are under democratic control? Are the operations of elected bodies and institutions sufficiently responsive to those who elect them? Are the processes of election sufficiently sensitive to reflect the true wishes of the electorate? Is there not more to democracy than elections? Should we not be concerned about the absence for so many people of involvement and participation in the political process? Are minorities – political, social, ethnic and so on – who are unlikely to be able to challenge the majority for overall political power, adequately protected? Is there not a danger that those who feel let down by democracy, who feel that they have insufficient control over the political process, will lose interest in the whole affair and will both signal and reinforce their powerlessness by opting out of democracy altogether, as they have done in large numbers in some other supposed democracies?

These questions raise large issues, which I do not propose to pursue at any length here. My purpose in raising them is merely to indicate that the diffusion of political power is not something that has been finally achieved, and that socialists must – in this field as in others – be aware of the constantly changing nature of the challenge that faces us.

I do, of course, draw some preliminary conclusions from the need to raise these questions. I conclude, for example, that there are important public functions that are not but should be exercised by democratically elected bodies. Health authorities, planning authorities, transport authorities, for example, are largely unelected and are beyond any direct democratic control. In other countries, and notably the United States, there is a much greater range of functions carried out by elected people; we do not have to endorse every aspect of their system to learn valuable lessons from them in the importance of bringing public functions closer to the people.

The socialist suspicion of concentrations of power dictates that power should be exercised always at the lowest possible level and on the smallest possible scale. Function should always determine the degree of power required to fulfil it, and the level at which that power should most appropriately be exercised. We should think much harder about the appropriate level at and form in which power should be exercised.

The presumption should always be that political power should be exercised at the minimum in terms of degree and level. The closer the exercise of power is to those affected, and the smaller its scale, the more easily controlled it is, and the more responsive it is to people's needs. We should not too easily assume that, because a function is carried out under the aegis of a democratically elected Government, that is all that has to be said in terms of democratic control and accountability.

There is therefore a powerful presumption for socialists in favour of decentralised power. In practical terms, British socialists should be concerned at the excessively centralised nature of political power in Britain – we are one of the most centralised states in the modern world – and should embrace for ideological as well as practical reasons the devolution of political power to the regions and localities, as part of the socialist programme for breaking down undue concentrations of power.

The revival of local government, in terms of both resources and powers, and the creation of a new tier of regional government, should be at the heart of any socialist reform of the political system. We have much to learn in this respect from the experience with regional government of more successful countries like West Germany.

The need to devolve power will become more urgent because it is contradicted and counter-acted by the need to create new institutions of political power at more remote and international levels. As argued above, the internationalisation of capital and the increased interdependence of national economies dictate the establishment of new, more comprehensive and more centralised political institutions. We should treat this – at least in terms of the diffusion of power – as a regrettable necessity, which takes power in the very direction it should not go. This makes it all the more important that we should make a conscious effort to identify and separate out those powers of government that inescapably have to be exercised at a high and remote level, and those that can appropriately be devolved to smaller-scale and more accessible institutions in local and regional government.

We should also be alert to the fact that elected institutions may be democratic in form but autocratic in practice. Power is no less concentrated simply because its provenance was the electoral process. Institutions of all kinds, democratic as well as others, have a natural tendency to elevate their own values, functions and very existence to an unchallengeable status. They protect themselves by exclusivities of various sorts – internal rules that are impenetrable to the outsider, an *esprit de corps* which creates a sense of separateness, a manipulation and evasion of attempts at external control.

In the case of democratic institutions, this natural tendency is reinforced by the response of those who find themselves excluded. Typically, those in whose hands the powers of democratic control rest in theory are easily deterred and respond to exclusion by disengagement and losing interest.

This means that we should be constantly critical of the institutions of political power, such as Parliament and local councils – critical not just of the substance of their decisions and actions, but also of their rules and procedures. These institutions themselves sometimes need protection against the subversion of their true purposes by others. Parliament, for example, has become notoriously the creature of the executive; the socialist must assert the need to strengthen the role of Parliament at the expense of the executive and should have little patience with those who argue that things cannot be done otherwise. The power of Prime Ministerial patronage, too, has become a real threat to the proper working of our democracy.

Equally, socialists should insist on reforms that are external to the political institutions – reforms like a Freedom of Information Act that would bring the actions of Government into more effective scrutiny, and reforms to the Press and broadcasting media that would encourage them to be more diverse and questioning and less subservient to Government.

It is also clear that minorities cannot be protected by the elective principle alone. Government by the majority, however carefully the majority's will is measured and given effect to, can simply become a means of oppression for the minority, unless their rights are protected independently of the electoral process. This is the basis of the case for fundamental human rights, which should depend not on membership of some politically dominant majority but on a concept of citizenship arising from the mere fact of belonging to society.


ELECTORAL REFORM

We should, however, be careful not to assume that all change is necessarily for the better. The question should always be – who will benefit from the change, and will it mean that the powerful acquire more power?

A case in point is so-called 'electoral reform'. The debate, such as it is, has so far followed a somewhat curious and one-sided course. All the running has been made by the reformers, who have managed as a result to imply that all the arguments for rationality and fairness are on their side, and that only the tired old Party hacks would wish – for obvious but discreditable reasons of self-interest – to defend the indefensible system we have at present.

Much is made of the apparent unfairness that the total number of votes, cast nationally, is not translated proportionately into numbers of seats. This apparently convincing argument is the basis of much of the agitation for some form of proportional representation (PR); yet it depends entirely on regarding elections as essentially national contests between political parties, rather than as opportunities for local communities to elect their representatives to send them to Westminster.

My point is not that one view is right and the other wrong (I am bound to concede that, however much we may wish that elections were still about communities sending representatives to the House of 'Commons' or communities, the nature of modern elections belies this essentially romantic interpretation); it is rather that the argument is not as simple as it is sometimes made out to be.

Judged by the socialist criterion that power should be diffused, proportional representation generally suffers a number of disadvantages, which must be set against the apparent gains in fairness and the more sensitive representation of diverse opinions and interests. Almost all systems of PR will mean a loss of direct representation (because of multi-member constituencies), or the elector's uncertainty as to the ultimate destination and purpose of his or her vote (because of transferable votes), or a significant increase in the power of Party officials to determine who should be elected (because of national or regional Party lists).

Each of these factors diminishes the power of the individual elector. Add to this the fact that most measures of electoral reform will mean the virtual inevitability of coalition Government (this is, in one sense, both their objective and their virtue) and there is then a further transfer of power from the individual to the politician or Party official. This arises because most coalitions are created by politicians as a consequence of negotiation rather than election. The ordinary voter has little chance to influence or predict the outcome of these negotiations, which typically take place far removed from the public gaze and after the votes have all been cast. They are entirely a matter for the politicians concerned.

The effects of coalition Government can also mean an unacceptable concentration of power, by placing unwarranted power in the hands of tiny and unrepresentative minorities, or alternatively by making it difficult if not impossible to remove large parties from power. This is what happened for most of the post-war period in Italy, and it is extremely dangerous, since it removes from the electorate the most fundamental of democratic rights – the power to throw one Government out and replace it with an alternative. It is the fact that our present two-Party, first-past-the-post system preserves this basic aspect of democracy that is its greatest strength.

My purpose in making these points is not to suggest that they are conclusive of the debate – there may well be stronger arguments in favour of reform where the objective is essentially a fair representation of views rather than the election of a Government, and there may also be variants, like the alternative vote, which overcome many of the objections to proportional representation – but merely to signal that the socialist should never lose sight of the fundamental objectives. It is not, in other words, an argument for making no change, but rather for being clear that change must promote the basic aim of diffusing power and increasing individual freedom and autonomy.

## A BILL OF RIGHTS

Similar considerations apply when addressing the question of entrenching human rights. As argued above, democratic procedures alone cannot guarantee to each citizen the basic rights and powers needed by each individual in a free society. That can be provided only by substantive provisions; and there are many who argue that even then the protection is too frail to withstand the will of the majority or the politicians' venality in search of the electoral support of that majority.

The argument is therefore advanced that basic provisions of the law concerning human rights should be entrenched against change or misinterpretation by giving them a special status – usually taking the form of a Bill of Rights. There is much to be said for this view, and the socialist should not be dismissive of the need to protect human rights against the demands of what has been called an 'elective dictatorship'. Again, however, we should be careful not to entrench power in remote or unrepresentative hands in the fond belief that we are thereby promoting freedom.

The fundamental difficulty for socialists with the concept of the Bill of Rights is that it means removing power from elected representatives (with all their frailties and deficiencies) and transferring it into the hands of judges who are neither elected nor likely to share the basic outlook of many of the citizens whose rights they are required to uphold.

This is not to say that the judges are anything other than independent and fearless upholders of the law. They are, however, as the record shows, likely to be more familiar with the value of property rights than with social security, more sympathetic to individual acquisitiveness than to community responsibility. They are essentially, valuably and inevitably, a force for conservatism in society.

There are other problems as well. A Bill of Rights that is framed in wide enough terms to offer protection to each citizen against all foreseeable abuses will inevitably be either too vague and general or will be subject to such exceptions (in favour of, for example, national security or emergency action) as to be difficult to enforce. In the British context there is the additional complication that the supremacy of Parliament – the fundamental principle of our constitution – makes it virtually impossible to entrench a Bill of Rights against subsequent amendment or enactments that are deliberately or by necessary implication inconsistent with it.

None of these arguments, persuasive though they are, should absolve us from the obligation to find an effective protection for human rights in our society. As we have seen, the dangers of the 'elective dictatorship' have become both more real and more apparent in recent years, and we should no longer take refuge in the old objections. Our task is to find solutions, not rehearse problems.

One widely canvasssed suggestion is that we should incorporate the European Convention on Human Rights (to which we
are already committed in international law and which includes a
right of individual petition to the European Commission and
Court of Human Rights) into domestic law. It may be that the
authority provided by its status in international law would
somehow help to entrench its provisions in domestic law; and it
may also be true that we are in the process of defining, in the
light of our membership of the EEC and our acceptance of the
supremacy of Community law, a new constitutional settlement
that will overcome some of the problems of giving a Bill of
Rights an inviolable status in British law.

For the time being, however, it may be wiser not to pin too
many hopes on a Bill of Rights, but to pursue instead a more
organically British solution. This should take the form of a
series of specific measures, designed to create enforceable
rights in every citizen and relying on the norm-setting impact of
legal provisions rather than on any special entrenched status in
order to achieve observance by Government, public authorities
and ordinary citizens.

The measures should include rights to obtain from public
authorities any information held concerning each individual,
rights to procedural fairness in respect of all decisions affecting
the individual and to full explanations of such decisions,
protections against all forms of discrimination, protections
against all forms of arbitrary treatment by public authorities,
rights to effective forms of redress against public authorities,
and substantive rights to minimum standards of income,
education, training, health care and housing.

The provision of specific and enforceable rights to each
individual in this way would create a legal revolution, which
would vastly increase the protection offered to the ordinary
citizen without having to confront the difficult constitutional
issues thrown up by a Bill of Rights. It is an essential part of the
socialist project.

THE NATURE OF POLITICAL POWER

For most political activists, the notion of political power is
usually seen as arising within a familiar landscape. Politics is

essentially a battle. The territorial prizes are the obvious ones –
the institutions of Government, whether central or local, and
other public bodies wielding quasi-governmental power. The
armies are the political parties, in which people enlist and serve
in an organised fashion, following leaders and pursuing
strategies. The weapons are the issues of political debate –
policies on the economy, or on health care, education or defence
– and the techniques of campaigning for electoral support.

For the activist, the battle is all-consuming. The armies surge
backwards and forwards, locked in perpetual combat. The air is
thick with the noise and smoke of battle. There are no
bystanders; everyone is involved. 'If you're not with us, you're
against us!' is the cry.

This is not the way politics seem to most people. For many of
them, politics is at best a sideshow, conducted at the margins of
their lives, by zealots who utter strange, ritualistic and barely
comprehensible noises, and who deserve attention only rarely,
at election time. The institutions of Government matter little to
them; the political parties are remote and unappealing and seem
to have more in common, in their bizarre rituals, with the gangs
or brotherhoods they read about but never encounter in their
everyday lives; and the issues and techniques of political
campaigning largely miss their intended targets by wide
margins.

To recognise this is not to endorse it. Of course, it would be
better if people felt that politics were more relevant to their
everyday lives, and it must be part of the socialist project to
bring this about. We do not make this more likely of
achievement, however, by misreading the reality and convincing ourselves that the battle is always against a committed
political enemy rather than for the support of the uncommitted.
This mistaken attitude can often alienate the very people whose
support we need and whose involvement we wish to encourage.

Misapprehensions about the perception of politics held by
ordinary people make it difficult for us to talk sensibly to them.
We are inclined to talk of involvement and participation as if
they are self-evidently desirable objectives. We imagine that
everyone wishes to have a say about everything.

We are not entirely wrong in these views. Where we make
our mistake, however, is in assuming that what people want is a
continuing involvement in formal political structures, and that

they wish to manipulate and influence the exercise of governmental power on a day-to-day and comprehensive basis. People do want to participate and to be involved, but on their terms – and those terms do not necessarily mean the sort of commitment to the endless meetings that are meat and drink to the political activist.

The participation most people want is the ability to delegate the normal tasks of Government to competent people who can be called to account from time to time. Where, however, the processes of Government impinge directly on the interests of the individual – whether personal and material or general and ethical – participation is not enough. Then, what is demanded from the political process is an immediate and relevant responsiveness, so that the individual can be satisfied that his or her view or interest is given proper weight.

We have to recognise that most people find their political involvement not in formal politics but instead in an informal structure of politics, which has little to do with the battleground so familiar to the political activist. Some of these informal structures will be recognisably, even if not formally, political. They will be single issue pressure groups, residents' associations, and, of course, trade unions and employers' associations.

Many others, however, will scarcely seem like political activities at all. They will be sports clubs, social arrangements, organising committees for festivals and carnivals. Their concerns will be women's issues and environmental questions, international relations and animal welfare, the cultural life and social affairs of ethnic minorities. These are the instruments that many ordinary people choose in order to pursue their aspirations and interests, and we should be foolish not to recognise that this form of politics has an equal legitimacy with the more familiar and formal kind.

What this means is that the more formal political processes have to accommodate this informal sub-structure of politics, by making themselves more available and accessible to those who will not wish to participate on a continuing basis but will demand immediate and effective access to the formal institutions when the need arises. This can be done partly through changes in those structures themselves, bringing them closer to people and their everyday lives through measures of devolution, by restoring the role and prestige of local government and by extending the elective principle to currently non-elected bodies.

But it must also be done by providing much greater support for the activities of voluntary organisations – through helping with meeting places and other facilities – and by making their access to the corridors of power easier and more direct. We must have more open Government and greater access to information. The aim must be a greater integration of the formal and voluntary aspects of political action.

Above all, we must make a much more determined effort to raise the level of political knowledge and awareness. The ignorance of most people in Britain about the political process and the functions of Government is a national disgrace and is an indictment of our educational system. For most people, 'Government' is an amorphous and confusing mass. They have little idea of who does what and with what authority. They have little idea of their rights and of the limits of governmental power. They assume both too much and too little – the one assumption being as damaging as the other. If we are to diffuse political power and make it a reality in the hands of ordinary people, we have to ensure that they are taught properly how the system works.

# CHAPTER TEN

# *A Socialism for the Future*

A huge effort has been made by our opponents over recent years to try to convince us that socialism is out-dated and backward-looking and cannot hope to meet the needs of modern society or the aspirations of the modern citizen. Much propaganda use has been made of the supposedly socialist models of Eastern Europe in order to discredit socialism and to represent it as necessarily inimical to individual freedom and economic success. The electoral success of the Right – in Britain, but elsewhere as well – has given added credibility to the attempt to engender a sense that socialism has had its day.

We have done little to help ourselves in the face of this onslaught. We have – in our rhetoric and attitudes – often seemed to confirm the travesty of socialism which our opponents wish to foist upon us. We have failed to develop a vision of the future to give the lie to the contention that we are out of touch with modern aspirations. We have paid little attention to the successful experience of other socialist societies, governments and parties – an experience which is of course studiously ignored by our opponents, but from which we could learn a great deal.

One factor that goes at least part of the way towards explaining our ineffectiveness is that we have suffered from a peculiar and almost paradoxical failure of ideological development. On the one hand, we have shown little interest in thinking about what our politics really mean and how they could develop; on the other hand, and partly as a consequence, we have allowed ourselves to become prisoners of an arid and sterile dogma that misrepresents our true purpose and inhibits us from making the effort to break free.

The result of accepting – at least in formal terms – an ideology in which we have little confidence is that we have allowed ourselves to direct our energies to goals that are unattainable and in any case undesirable; that we damage our self-confidence by having to denigrate our achievements as being inconsistent with our ideological objectives; and that we cut ourselves off from and are suspicious of new thinking and more hopeful lines of development.

The time has come to free ourselves from these shackles and to develop and promote a new socialism which is manifestly suited to the needs of a modern industrial society. The socialism I have tried to outline here, taking as its base and central aim the diffusion of power in society, is well suited, I believe, to meet both social and individual interests in the modern world.

It is the one political doctrine to give proper and equal weight to every individual, and to recognise the importance of the contribution that each individual can make to society. It therefore frees us immediately from the problems we have sometimes imagined ourselves to have in responding to individual success and ambition. We can unreservedly welcome individual achievements and aspirations, subject only to the crucial proviso that the encouragement must be for every individual, and that one individual's success must not be at the expense of others.

The true doctrine of the individual offers to everyone the chance of securing what Rawls calls the most important primary good – self-esteem. It places clear limitations on the permissible encroachments on individual freedoms attempted not only by other individuals but also by State and collective power. It provides a secure doctrinal foundation for the insistence on equal rights, and for the outlawing of discrimination of all sorts.

Many socialists may, of course, feel uncomfortable with a doctrine which seems to place such emphasis on the individual. It is true that there is little here of class conflict, or of the attempt to locate and identify the individual primarily in relation to class. The diffusion of power, and the emphasis on the worth of each individual, is, however, entirely consistent with the socialist purpose, and provides valuable gains to the socialist cause.

It means, for example, that while proper weight is given to the importance of individual striving (something other attempts at socialism have at times tried to devalue, though in vain), the social value given to each individual provides a substantial counterweight to this potentially aggressive and competitive factor, and ensures that society is seen as essentially a co-operative, communal and non-conflictual enterprise to which each person contributes.

Most important, the individual is securely placed in the social context. It is not just that social action is recognised as necessary for the full realisation of each individual's potential; nor is it just that collective action is recognised as essential if some individuals are not to be unfairly penalised by the excessive power of others. It is also a recognition that society alone can provide the rules and conditions that will allow certain intangibles – of great importance to a full life and to individual satisfaction – to be guaranteed. Those intangibles are the social virtues of tolerance, compassion, responsibility and morality, which can come only from a society that is cohesive and functioning well – and to this must be added the sense of individual satisfaction derived from participating in a successful joint enterprise.

A modern socialism is not only well attuned to individual aspirations and to the meeting of social responsibilities to the individual. It is also the best way for society to function in terms of achieving success, not just for an agglomeration of individuals but for society as a whole. That success will often be measured in economic terms. In seeking economic success, a modern socialism is able to utilise the market and take the best advantage of its strengths, while at the same time making good the market's deficiencies by using the community's resources and organising power to give effect to the longer-term and wider view, essential to success in a modern economy.

Working co-operatively to supplement and over-ride the market is not, of course, uniquely socialist. There are many economies that are far from being socialist where action of this sort is regarded as axiomatic. The particular contribution which socialists can make is not just the recognition that the market needs to be supplemented and over-ridden in this way, but also that the attempt to do so gives rise to the dangers of corporatism, which must also be overcome.

A modern socialism, by diffusing not just political power but economic power as well, will reduce the danger that engaging both the political and economic power in society to the achievement of joint social ends will concentrate power in too few hands. It will recognise both the importance of making this collective effort and the danger it poses to the freedoms of the ordinary citizen. That danger has been clearly demonstrated, not only in the so-called socialist countries of Eastern Europe and China, where political power predominates, but also – perhaps less obviously – in capitalist countries where political power is subservient to those with economic power.

The socialism I advocate also provides us with a secure ideological foundation from which to confront social and political problems that might arise in the future but that we cannot foresee, or can discern only dimly, at present. We already know that a socialist insistence on the diffusion of power, on the value of each individual and on the importance of society, equips us to deal with emerging issues such as the proper role of women, the power of new technology, the internationalisation of capital and the threat to the environment. There will, however, be other issues in the future to which we will not have ready-made answers; a sound political starting-point will help us to make the right responses.

We should not expect, of course, that we shall ever be able to resolve all our problems. Society and the issues it throws up are infinitely variable, and perfect solutions are the stuff of political theses rather than real life. All we can hope for is that we should equip ourselves to grapple with those problems, of the present and the future, by adopting a body of principle which is humane, optimistic and resourceful, and which offers the highest goals to the human spirit.

# Bibliography

A. Smith: *The Wealth of Nations* (London, 1776)

P.-J. Proudhon: *Qu'est-ce que la Propriété?* (Paris, 1840)

F. Hayek: *The Road to Serfdom* (London, 1944)

R.H. Tawney: *Equality* (London, 1952)

C.A.R. Crosland: *The Future of Socialism* (London, 1956)

J. Rawls: *A Theory of Justice* (London, 1972)

R. Nozick: *Anarchy, State and Utopia* (Oxford, 1974)

C. Lindblom: *Politics and Markets* (New York, 1977)

Report of the Bullock Committee Inquiry: *Industrial Democracy* (London, 1977)

A. Nove: *The Economics of Feasible Socialism* (London, 1983)

B. Gould: *Socialism and Freedom* (London, 1985)

*Index on Censorship* (London, 1988)

Labour Party: *Aims and Values* (London, 1988)

W. McCarthy: *The Future of Industrial Democracy* (London, 1988)

D. Marquand: *The Unprincipled Society* (London, 1988)

M. Smith: *Consumers and the Community* (London, 1988)

J. Le Grand and S. Estrin, ed.: *Market Socialism* (London, 1989)

# Index

Agriculture, Ministry of, and food scares 166
*Aims and Values* (Labour Party) 94

Bank of England, power 83–4
banks, *see* financial institutions
Barrowfield, Glasgow, community business 166
BBC, independence 46
benefit, social security 39–40
Bill of Rights 178–80
Britain: decline xi; and international economy 8–9
British Telecom, re-nationalisation 128–9
broadcasting media, bullied 46–7
Bullock Report 151–2

Callaghan, James 8, 84
capital: and credit 10–11; internationalisation of 6–9, 32–7, 52; ownership of 11–15, 117; power 32–7
capitalism: British 1–3; corporate 13–14; new 9–15, 59; power, diffusion 14–15, 135; strength of 9
centralisation, excessive 46, 50–2
choice, power of 63, 64–7, 173; and collective provision 169–70
Churchill, Winston 82
citizenship 71–2; active 70
City, the, *see* financial institutions
Civil Service 48, 83
class: sense of, disappearance 21–2; war 21
coalition Government 177–8
Cole, G.D.H. 74
collective provision: accountability 167–72; and choice 65, 169–70; testing 168–9
common ownership: across the economy 134, 135–6; decentralised forms 56; public sector 120–2, 134

community businesses 165–6
Community Health Councils 170–1
companies: members of 152; worker ownership 137–43
company law, changes 149–53
compensation, and public ownership 128–30
competition, market 161–3
Confederation of British Industry 84, 86–7
Conservative Party: credibility 56–7; support 25, 27; *see also* Thatcherism
consumer boom 31–2
consumers: and collective provision 169; control 171; importance 158–9, 169; information 166; in market 108; ombudsman for 167; ownership 163–6; protection 161–3, 166–7; rational choice 99, 169–70, 171; right of redress 167; and utilities 159–61
co-operative enterprise 137, 142–3, 163–4
corporatism 88
council house sales 19–20
credit, increasing 10–11
credit unions 164–5
Crosland, Anthony 1–3, 6–7, 9–10, 14, 15, 21, 24, 58, 76
Cuomo, Mario 146

decentralisation 55–6; of utilities 123
democracy: and political power 173–6; and public bodies 174, 175–6; true 35–6
Devon Health Service, locality planning 172
disadvantaged people: and house prices 38–9; and market 101–2; morality of 69; rights, diminution 39–40; and Thatcherism 26–7
discrimination, Right-wing 53–4
domestic employment 79

economy: changing 15–17, 135; common ownership 134–7; failure 28–32; imperial 82; international 7–9; macro-economic measures 80–1; organisation of 80–5; success 77
elderly people, community care 172
elective dictatorship 45, 179
electoral reform 176–8
employee ownership, see worker ownership
employee share ownership plans (esops) 138, 143–9; democratic 146–7
employment, full 2, 77–9; and diffusion of power 78; and inflation 5; unattainable 6
enterprise culture 68–9
enterprises: members of 152; worker ownership 137–43
environment: and collective provision 110–11; concern for 54
equity: ownership of 11–12; public ownership 128–30
esops, see employee share ownership plans
Estrin, S. 96, 105
European Convention on Human Rights 180
European Economic Community 7; single market 31, 34–5
exchange rate 83

Falklands conflict 24
Finance Act (1989) 145
financial institutions: and control of capital 11, 12, 13–14; priority given to 32, 33, 82–3, 84; and privatisation 39; regulation 40; and morality 69
Fordism 15–17
freedom: assault on 45–50; and choice 63
Freedom of Information Act 176
Freeman, James 147, 148

Golden Shares 130–1, 132
Gold Standard 34, 81, 82, 84
Gorbachev, Mikhail 56
government: coalition 177–8; democracy in 176; and State, interests 48

Hailsham, Lord 45
Hayek, F. 49
Healey, Denis 56, 84
health care: choice in 169–71; and market 109–10; monitoring 171

Hodder, Alex 147–9
housing: council house sales 19–20; supply 19–20; value of 38–9, 115–16; tenure, form 20, 65

Independent Broadcasting Authority (IBA) 46–7
Independent Labour Party 58
*Index on Censorship* 45
individual, the: choice 64–7; power 62; self-esteem 63, 69, 78, 185; socialist view of 185–6, 187; and society 67, 72
Industrial Common Ownership Movement 142
industrial democracy 150–3; and economic performance 151
industry 28–9; competitiveness 30, 41; government co-operation with 86, 87–8; internationalisation 35, 36; investment in 31, 41–2, 89; new strategy 85–9; new technology 41–2; research and development 31, 89; training in 31, 42, 89; wider ownership 117
inflation 29–30
information: consumer provision 166–7; freedom of 176; as power 42–3; restricted 47–8
institutional entrepreneurship 157
insurance companies, and capital 10, 11
interest rates 32
Italy, coalition Government 178

Japan, government-industry co-operation 86

Kent Community Care Scheme 171–2
Keynesianism, demise of 5–6

labelling, standards 166
labour, organised 2, 6, 7; and new technology 41–2
Labour Party: and British Telecom 128–9; Constitution, Clause Four 120–1; countering Thatcherism 55; and financial establishment 84–5; and full employment 79; housing policy 19–20; indecisiveness 64; internal conflict 23–4, 64; out-of-date 15, 16–17, 18–21, 111, 184; Policy Review xv; and success 74–5, 77; support 22, 23, 59; and working class 22; see also socialism
laissez-faire policies 60–1, 104

Lancashire Enterprise Board 157
law, domestic, and European
  Convention on Human Rights 180
Le Grand, J. 96, 105
limited liability companies 149–50
limited return companies 152–3
Lindblom, C. 106, 107, 112
local authorities: and consumer
  protection 167; democratic role 175;
  housing policy 19–20; and local
  economy 136, 156–7; regional
  enterprise boards 156–7; restriction
  on 39, 46, 136; services, satisfactory
  169; user control 171
Local Government Act, 1988 (Section
  28) 48

McCarthy, Lord 151
MacDonald, Ramsay 8, 84
Manpower Services Commission 167
manufacturing, see industry
market, the: advantages of 95–6, 106–7,
  112; balance of power in 108–9;
  capriciousness of 56, 99, 103; and
  'catching up' 105–6; and choice 65,
  103; competition 161–3; deficiencies
  98–107, 109–11; as exchange
  mechanism 101–2, 106–7; flexible
  approach to 112; inappropriate
  mechanism 109–12; and insurance
  104; intervention in 97–8, 100, 101,
  102, 108, 111; as means of organising
  society 106–7; and price changes
  103–4; public goods in 100, 101,
  110–11; short-term view 105; in
  socialist states 94; unfairness 102–3
Marquand, David 106, 111
Marxism: invalidity 1, 2, 9, 13, 14; and
  Labour Party 22; and property 115
material advance, drive 76
Maxwell, Robert 13, 43
media: concentration of power in 42–4;
  restrictions on 46–7
membership companies 152–3
mergers, see takeovers and mergers
Merseyside Enterprise Board 157
Mitterand, François 8
Mondragon 141, 142, 157
monetarism: abandoned 29, 33, 56;
  emergence 5–6
monopoly, utilities as 123–4, 159
morality, differing standards 69
Morris, William 58

Murdoch, Rupert 44

Nanny State 49
National Economic Development
  Council (NEDC) 86
National Health Service (NHS) 2; and
  choice 65, 169–70; and market
  mechanism 110
nationalisation 2, 121; disappointing
  performance 121–2; see also public
  ownership
News International 44–5
North Sea oil, economic benefits 3,
  24–5, 29, 30–1
Norway, North Sea oil 30
Nove, Alec 100
Nozick, R. 49

Official Secrets Acts 47–8
Oftel 171
ombudsmen, provision 167
Owen, Robert 58
ownership 113–18; common 120–1, 122,
  134–7; compensation 128–9, 130;
  employee 137–43; modification
  119–20; public 120–3, 123–6, 127,
  133, 135; and shareholding 127–8,
  130–3

Parliament, and the executive 176
patronage: political 48; prime
  ministerial 176
Peacock Commission 47
pension funds 10, 11, 136; social
  ownership 153–4; wage-earner funds
  155–6
Pensions and Investment Resource
  Centre 154
People's Provincial bus company 147–9
political power: concentration of 174–5,
  187; diffusion 173–4, 175; nature of
  180–3
Post Office, worker representation
  151–2
power: concentration of 42–5, 51–2,
  60–1; diffusion of 60–3, 66, 74, 78,
  117, 134, 144, 186, 187; in market
  108–9; political 173–6, 180–3;
  and property 116–17
press: concentration of power in 42–4;
  restrictions on 47

privatisation: and common ownership 122–3; failure of 122; and privilege 39–40; reversal of 127, 128
privilege, reinforcement of 37–40
productivity, improved 41–2
property, private 113–18; confiscation 128–30; and power 116–17
proportional representation 177
prosperity, attitudes to 74–7
Proudhon, P.-J. 113
public ownership 120–3, 123–6, 127, 133, 135
public spending 29

Rawls, J. 61, 63, 69, 185
regional enterprise boards 156–7
regional policy: abandoned 51; Labour strategy 55–6
Right, the: changes in 56–7; swing to 4–5
rights: Bill of 178–80; diminution 39–40, 45

savings: and equity capital 10, 11, 117
Scandinavia, user control in 171
Securities and Investment Board 40
self-esteem 63, 69, 78, 185
Shah, Eddie 44
shares: employee holdings 137–43; Government holdings 127–8, 130–3; ownership 39, 144
Smith, Adam 97, 104
Smith, Martin 172
Social Democratic Party 24
Socialism: achievements of 2; attributes of xiii–xv, 59; decline, arresting 57–8; flexibility 136; future 58–9, 60, 66, 72, 184–7; ideological base 58, 184, 187
*Socialism and Freedom* (Gould) 60
society: denial of 67, 70; importance of 67–72, 187; and the individual 186
Soviet Union, market mechanism 94
*Spycatcher* affair 47
State: and business community 107; developmental 106, 111; interests, and Government 48; minimalist 49–50, 68
sterling, maintaining 83–5
stock market crash (1987) 2, 56
Strathclyde Community Business Ltd 166
success, attitudes to 74–7

Sweden, wage-earner funds 155

takeovers and mergers 40; and industrial democracy 151; tough approach to 162–3
Tawney, R.H. 61, 62
tax changes, regressive 37
technology, new 41–2; and full employment 78–9; and the media 43
Thatcherism: blind spots 52–4; and British decline xi–xii; and centralisation 51–2; environmental issues 54; extreme 57; failure xii, 3, 26, 28; ideology xii–xiii; and individual choice 64, 65–6; and the market 56; and minimalist state 49–50; North Sea oil 24–5, 57; opportunistic 4–5; political agenda 57; and society 67–8; women's rights 53
Trade and Industry, Department of 86
trades unions 2, 3; closed shop 91–3; and economic policy 90, 93; and esops 146–7; government relationship with 89–93; legal immunity 90–1; outdated 16; restrictive measures 39, 46
trust law 153–4

unemployment 3; creation of 78–9; and poverty 78
Unity Trust bank 145–6, 149, 164
University Grants Commission 46
user control 171
utilities: controlling shareholding 127–8, 130–3; decentralisation 123; economic importance 125; investment in 126; as natural monopolies 123–4, 159; public ownership 123–6, 127; regulating 159–61; social function 124–5

wage-earner funds 154–6
wealth: attitudes to 74–7; and choice 39; creators of 80, 81; and property 38–9, 115–16; redistribution 116, 118; surplus 117
Welfare State 2, 3; and inflation 5
West Midlands Enterprise Board 157
Wilson, Harold 22, 84
women, role in society 53
worker ownership 137–43, 150; esops 143–9; individual stakes 139–41; and outside finance 141–2, 143; profit sharing 141–2; voting rights 141
working class, class sense 21–2